First World War

and Army of Occupation

War Diary

France, Belgium and Germany

47 DIVISION
140 Infantry Brigade
London Regiment
8th (City of London) Battalion (Post Office Rifles)
5 July 1915 - 1 November 1915

WO95/2731/1

The Naval & Military Press Ltd
www.nmarchive.com
Published in association with The National Archives

Published by

The Naval & Military Press Ltd

Unit 10 Ridgewood Industrial Park,

Uckfield, East Sussex,

TN22 5QE England

Tel: +44 (0) 1825 749494

www.naval-military-press.com

www.nmarchive.com

This diary has been reprinted in facsimile from the original. Any imperfections are inevitably reproduced and the quality may fall short of modern type and cartographic standards.

Contents

Operation(al) Order(s)	Operation Order No. 11 by Brigadier General G.J. Cuthbert, C.B., Commanding 140th Infantry Bde.	18/06/1918	18/06/1918
Miscellaneous			
Operation(al) Order(s)	Operation Order No. 12 140th Infantry Brigade.	13/06/1915	13/06/1915
Miscellaneous			
Operation(al) Order(s)	Operation Order No. 15 by Brigadier General G.J. Cuthbert, C.B., Commanding 140th Infantry Brigade.	20/06/1915	20/06/1915
Miscellaneous			
Operation(al) Order(s)	Operation Order No. 14. 140th Infantry Brigade.	21/06/1915	21/06/1915
Miscellaneous			
Operation(al) Order(s)	Operation Order No. 15. 140th Infantry Brigade.	25/06/1915	25/06/1915
Miscellaneous			
Miscellaneous	A Form Messages And Signals.		
Miscellaneous			
Operation(al) Order(s)	Operation Order No. 16. 140th Infantry Brigade.	26/06/1915	26/06/1915
Miscellaneous			
Operation(al) Order(s)	Operation Order No. 17 140th Infantry Bde.	27/06/1918	27/06/1918
Miscellaneous			
Operation(al) Order(s)	Operation Order No. 2. by Brigadier General G.J. Cuthbert, C.B., Commanding 140th Infantry Bde.	01/06/1915	01/06/1915
Miscellaneous			
Map	Index To Numbers On 1:10,000 Map.		
Miscellaneous			
Map	Index To Numbers On 1:5,000 Map.		
Map	La Bassee		
Miscellaneous	La Basse 1/5000		
Miscellaneous			
Map			
Map	Festubert		
Miscellaneous			
Heading	140th Bde. 47th Div. War Diary 1/8th London Regt. July 1915		
Miscellaneous	On His Majesty's Service.		
Heading	47th Division 8th Div Lon Regt. Vol V From 1st to 31st July 1915		
Miscellaneous			
Operation(al) Order(s)	Operation Order No. 18. 140th Infantry Brigade.	01/07/1915	01/07/1915
Miscellaneous			
Operation(al) Order(s)	Operation Order No. 19. 140th Infantry Brigade.		
Miscellaneous			
Miscellaneous		05/07/1915	05/07/1915
Miscellaneous			
Operation(al) Order(s)	Operation Order No. 20. 140th Infantry Brigade.		
Miscellaneous			
Operation(al) Order(s)	Operation Order No. 21. 140th Infantry Brigade.	29/07/1915	29/07/1915
Miscellaneous			
Operation(al) Order(s)	142 Infantry Brigade. Operation Order No. 24	27/06/1915	27/06/1915
Miscellaneous			
Operation(al) Order(s)	142nd Infantry Brigade Operation Order Number 28	06/07/1918	06/07/1918
Miscellaneous			
Heading	140th Bde. 47th Div. War Diary 1/8th London Regt. August 1915		
Miscellaneous	On His Majesty's Service.		
Heading	47th Division 1/8th London Regt Vol VI 1-31.8.15		
Miscellaneous			
Operation(al) Order(s)	140th Infantry Brigade Preliminary Notice of Relief.	31/07/1915	31/07/1915

Miscellaneous			
Operation(al) Order(s)	Operation Order No. 22		
Operation(al) Order(s)	Operation Order No. 22. 140th Infantry Brigade.	01/08/1915	01/08/1915
Miscellaneous			
Miscellaneous	140th Infantry Brigade Schedule of Reliefs.		
Miscellaneous			
Miscellaneous	140th Infantry Brigade. Working Parties for night of 1st-2nd August, 1915.	02/08/1915	02/08/1915
Miscellaneous			
Miscellaneous	140th Infantry Brigade. Machine Guns.		
Miscellaneous	Preliminary Operation Order.	24/08/1915	24/08/1915
Miscellaneous			
Miscellaneous	140th Infantry Brigade.	25/08/1915	25/08/1915
Miscellaneous			
Operation(al) Order(s)	Operation Order No. 23 140th Infantry Brigade.	24/08/1915	24/08/1915
Miscellaneous			
Heading	140th Bde. 47th Division. War Diary 1/8th London Regiment. September 1915		
Miscellaneous			
Miscellaneous	8th-13th London Rgt. Post Office Rifle.		
Miscellaneous			
Diagram etc			
Miscellaneous	Twenty Ninth Div.		
Miscellaneous			
Heading	140th Bde. 47th Div. War Diary 1/8th London Regt. October 1915		
Miscellaneous	On His Majesty's Service.		
Heading	47th Division 1/8th London Regt. Vol VIII Oct 15		
Miscellaneous			
Miscellaneous	8th Bn London Regt. (Post Office Rifles). War Diary October.	01/11/1915	01/11/1915
Miscellaneous	To Accompany War Diary October 1915		
Operation(al) Order(s)	Operation Order No. 31 by Brigadier General G.J. Cuthbert, C.B.	08/10/1915	08/10/1915
Miscellaneous			
Operation(al) Order(s)	140th Infantry Brigade Operation Order No. 31.	11/10/1915	11/10/1915
Miscellaneous			
Operation(al) Order(s)	140th Infantry Brigade. Operation Order No. 34.	21/10/1915	21/10/1915
Operation(al) Order(s)	140th Infantry Brigade. Operation Order No. 35	26/10/1915	26/10/1915
Miscellaneous			
Operation(al) Order(s)	140th Infantry Brigade. Operation Order No. 36.	29/10/1915	29/10/1915
Miscellaneous			

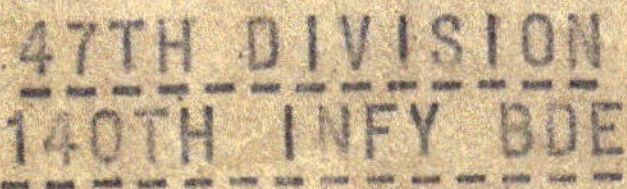

1-8TH LONDON REGIMENT

MAR 1915 - JAN 1918

JAN 1918

To 58 DIV
174 BDE

PUBLIC RECORD
OFFICE

378 END -

141st Infantry Brigade

20th Battalion Lon Regt

Handing over Statement - XI - 30th July 1915

	LEFT COY.	CENTRE COY.	RIGHT COY.	KEEPS.	HEADQUARTERS	TOTAL.
SAA In Boxes.	61000.	48000.	64600.	141000		314600.
Bombs Battey	160.	150	225	1218		1753
" Mills						
" No 9				174		174
Very Pistols						
" lights	126	80	60	480	120	866
Periscopes Box						
" Vigilant						
" Folding						
Scaling ladders	6	11	9	MINING 12		26
Picks	50	25	25	77	2	MINING 179
Shovels	50	25	25	68 MINING 6		168
Mudscoops.	-	2			3	5
Sickles	4	4	4			12
Wire Barbed	8	10	6	1	35	60
" Plain or French.	4	2	3	1	14	24
Vermorel Sprayers.	3	2	1	4		
Solution for above	Bolts: 3	Tins 1	Tins 3	Tins 4 Bottles 6		
Sandbags.	300	50	200	630	1200	2380
Grenades rifle	-		40			40
Loopholes.	43		6			49
Buckets, Canvas	18	9	12		16	55
" Latrine	5		5			10
Maul.	2	1		1		4
Rockets	12	12	12	24	12	72
" Sticks	6	6	6	12	11	41
" Stand	1	1	1	4	1	8
Pickets long.	50	60			(Iron) 17	127
Staples	100					100
Saws, hand	2			1		3
Hammers	2				1	3
Shovels French			3		7	12
Scrapers.			7			7
Scythes.			6			6
Sandbag cradle			1			1
Wire netting					1	1
Catapults					2	2
Handles					34	34
Mortars, Signal					1	1
Signals					4	4
Taps.				6		6
Vent pegs.				6		6
Chevaux de frise.				8		8
Barrels				8		8
Gooseberries				23 / 532	3	26 / 502
Bully Beef.				Tins 18		18
Biscuits [illegible]				20		20

140th Bde.

47th Div.

Battn. disembarked Havre from England 18.3.15

WAR DIARY

1/8th LONDON REGT.

MARCH

1 9 1 5

On His Majesty's Service.

2

121/48⁰/4

1/4 London Brigade

8th Co: of London.

Vol I. 17 – 31. 3. 15

PUBLIC RECORD

140th Bde.
47th Div.

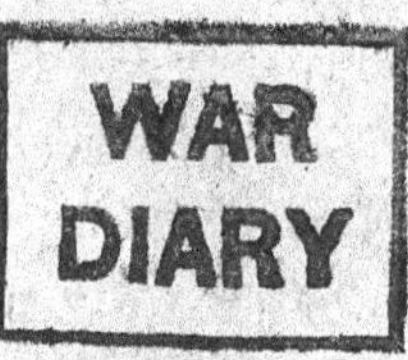

1/8th LONDON REGT.

APRIL

1 9 1 5

Attached:
140th Inf. Bde O.Os
Nos. 2 + 3
4th Gds Bde O.O. No. 10.

On His Majesty's Service.

15

2nd London Division

1/18th London Regt.

Vol II 1–30.4.15.

Copy No. 6.

Operation Order No. 2
by
Brigadier General G. J. Cuthbert, C.B.,
Commanding 4th London Infantry Brigade.

12th April, 1915.

Information. 1. The Brigade will move into billets at BURBURE and ALLOUVARGNE today.

Detail. 2. (a) The Brigade Headquarters, 8th and 7th Bns. London Regiment will move to ALLOUVARGNE and be billeted there. These Units with 1st and 2nd Line Transport will pass the level crossing E. of AUCHEL on the AUCHEL-LOZINGHEM road at 1·45 p.m., 2 p.m. and 2·45 p.m. respectively.

(b) The 6th Bn. London Regiment, with 1st and 2nd Line Transport will move to BURBURE and be billeted there. They will leave RAIMBERT at 2 p.m. and will march independently.

(c) The 4th London Field Ambulance will leave AUCHEL at 2·45 p.m. and go into billets at BURBURE moving by RAIMBERT.

Reports. 3. Brigade Headquarters will close at 12·30 p.m. and will reopen at ALLOUVARGNE on arrival there.

R. Tempest. Major,
Brigade Major,
4th London Infantry Brigade

Issued at 9·30 a.m.

Copy No. 1. - War Diary.
2. - Operation Order File.
3. - O.C. 6th Bn. London Regt. by Signal Section.
4. - O.C. 7th Bn. London Regt. " "
5. - O.C. 8th Bn. London Regt. " "
6. - O.C. 4th Lon. Field Ambce. " "

8
PUBLIC RECORD
OFFICE

SECRET. No. 5

OPERATION ORDER No. 3

by

Brigadier General W.J.Cuthbert, C.B.,

Commanding 4th London Infantry Brigade.

LE PREOL.(F10a)
23rd April, 1915.

Reference Map- Combined Sheet-
France - BETHUNE.

INTENTION.1. The Battalions of the Brigade will rejoin the Brigade to-morrow, 24th April, 1915, and will move into billets at LABEUVRIERE and LAPUGNOY.

DETAIL. 2. (i) The Brigade will move in two columns -

Column A - Brigade Headquarters, 6th Bn.London Regt., 7th Bn.London Regt. - Commander, Colonel Faux, 7th Bn.London Regt. This column will pass the starting point - level crossing at E4a at 12 noon, and march via CHOCQUES and go into billets as follows:- 6th and 7th Battalions at LAPUGNOY. Brigade Headquarters Chateau at LABEUVRIERE.

Column B - 8th Bn.London Regt., 15th Bn.London Regt. Commander, Colonel Kenny, 15th Bn.London Regt., will pass the starting point - Church at BEUVRY at 11.30 a.m. and will march via BEUVRY-RUE DE LILLE-RUE DE LETOUR-RUE D'AIRE-level crossing E4a-CHOCQUES, and will be billeted at LABEUVRIERE.

(ii) Blanket wagons of the Train will accompany Units.

(iii) Billeting parties will meet the Staff Captain as follows- 6th and 7th Battalions at the MAIRIE, LAPUGNOY, at 11.30 a.m. 8th and 15th Battalions at the MAIRIE, LABEUVRIERE, at 11 a.m.

(iv) Brigade Headquarters will close at LE PREOL at 1 p.m. and will reopen at CHATEAU LABEUVRIERE.

R. Tempest
Major,
Brigade Major.
4th London Infantry Brigade.

9
PUBLIC RECORD OFFICE

Issued at 8-30 p.m.

Copy No.1 - - - - - War Diary.

,, 2 - - - - - Operation Order File.

,, 3 - - - - - C.O. 6th Battalion. By Orderly.

,, 4 - - - - - C.O. 7th ,, ,,

,, 5 - - - - - C.O. 8th ,, ,,

,, 6 - - - - - C.O.[illegible]th ,, ,,

NOTE. To be acknowledged by bearer.

<u>SECRET.</u>

OPERATION ORDERS <u>No. 10.</u>

by

Brigadier General G.J.CUTHBERT. C.B.,

Commanding 4th Guards Brigade.

22nd April 1915.

Reference combined sheet
BETHUNE 1/40000.

---

1. Under instructions 1st Corps, the Command of the front now held by the 2nd Division will be handed over to G.O.C. London Division at 10 a.m. on 24th April. By that hour the line will be held as follows:-

A1 Section CUINCHY 3rd Bn. Coldstream Guards.

A2 Section CUINCHY 2nd Bn. Coldstream Guards.

B1 Section GIVENCHY 1st Bn. Herts. Regiment.

B2 Section GIVENCHY 1st Bn Irish Guards.

B3 Section GIVENCHY <u>2nd</u> Bn Grenadier Guards.

Festubert Section 5th London Inf. Brigade.

2. Colonel Feilding D.S.O. will Command the CUINCHY sub-section and will relieve the troops of the 6th Inf. Brigade in this section on the 24th April. Details of this relief will be arranged direct between Colonel Feilding. D.S.O. and the 6th Inf. Brigade.

3. All trench stores including Mortars will be handed over to the relieving Units.

4. Troops of the 4th London Brigade affiliated to 4th Guards Brigade will be withdrawn from the front line tomorrow 23rd and the following reliefs will take place:-

<u>B1 Section</u> 1st Herts will relieve 15th London the latter will move into billets at LE PREOL.

No troops of 1st Herts Regt. will be East of Brigade Headquarters before 6 p.m.

/ / .

Sheet 2.

B3 Section. 2nd Bn Grenadier Guards will relieve 8th London.

The latter will move into billets at LE QUESNOY.

The 2nd Bn Grenadiers Guards will leave BETHUNE 2-30 p.m. to relieve 8th London. Route:-

BOULEVARD VICTOR HUGO - MARCHE d s CHEVAUX

and South bank of Canal.

5. 4th Field Ambulance will take over the evacuation of the CUINCHY section in addition to the GIVENCHY section from 10a.m. 24th April.

6. Brigade Report centre unch nged.

Gort Captain.

Bde Major, 4th Guards Brigade.

Copy No 1 2nd Bn Grenadier Guards.
No 2 2nd Bn Coldstream Guards.
No 3 3rd Bn Coldstream Guards.
No 4 1st Bn Irish Guards.
No 5 1st Bn Hertfordshire Regiment.
No 6 8th London.
No 7 18th London.
No 8 Office Copy.
No 9 War Diary.
No 10. 4 London Inf Bde

Acknowledge by wire

12

27 continued

During the 24th - 25th - 26th the losses of the Bn were as follows

	Officers	Other Ranks	
K.	3	42	Total 10. 272
W	5	222	
Missing or Died of wounds	2	4	

28. Bn in Brigade Reserve at the Turning Fork.

29. - 30 30. The Bn found a working party at night of 7 Officers & 200 men.
3 Other Ranks were wounded.

30. Bn remained in Brigade Reserve at the Turning Fork under orders to move at short notice.

Total Casualties to Date

	Officers	Other Ranks
K	4	57
W	8	302
Missing or Died of Wounds.	3	5

[signature]
Capt [illegible]

60

NCO's & Rfn Brought before the Commanding Officer for Good Service

At GIVENCHY 23. 4. 15

No 591 Sgt Brand (1) Controlling his section well when under shell fire

No 1490 a/c C P Long (1)

No 1545 Rfn A E Thompson (1)

No 1509 Rfn W. ~~Holland~~ Howard (3)

No 1699 Rfn CW Rushforth (3)

When employed as Stretcher Bearers carrying out their duties with skill & coolness under fire

At Festhubert 10 – 21 May

Runners & Stretcher Bearers

No 1 Coy

1425	Rfn Warwick SJ	1359	Rfn Staples EL
1920	" Hasant FW	1509	" Howard WT
2169	" Mattock CA	2697	" Forster W
2204	" Goodsall HO	2434	" Rogers E
1611	Knight CW		

No 2 Coy

14	Coy Sgt Maj Radley J	2644	Rfn Cole WG
520	Sgt Aberdeen AW	1960	" Harris W
778	" Weaver C	1830	" Jenner J
1551	a/c Burnett	1570	" Walton AE
		2533	Rfn Jenny JA

140th Bde.
47th Div.

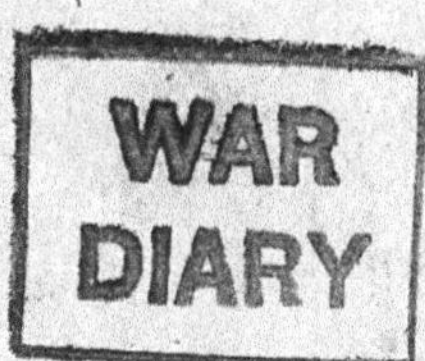

1/8th L O N D O N REGT.

MAY

1 9 1 5

On His Majesty's Service.

19

140/

121/5481

47th Division.

8th London Regt.

Vol III 1—30.5.15

140th Bde.
47th Div.

1/8th LONDON REGT.

JUNE

1 9 1 5

attached:
140th Inf. Bde
OOs Nos. 9 (c)
Maps.

On His Majesty's Service.

War Diary
8th Bn London Regt Post Office Rifles.
June 1915

June 1st The Bn received orders to move to billets at BETHUNE at 4pm
En route the Bn was stopped & received orders to move to VERMELLES.
The Bn took over Y2 Section of the defences from the London Scottish. Nos 1.3.4. Coys being in the trenches No 2 in Support.

2nd
3rd } Lt Vince rejoined for duty. Bn remained in the Trenches as above.
4th
5th
6th

7th The Bn was relieved in the evening by the S. Staffordshire Regt & marched to NOEUX-LES-MINES arriving there at daybreak on the 8th. The whole Bn formed the Divisional Reserve.

8
9 } The Bn remained at NOEUX-LES-MINES
10
11

12 The Bn was visited in the afternoon by the Rt. Hon. Herbert Samuel Post Master General.
The Bn left its billets in the evening being relieved by the 18th London Regt & moved to billets at LE PHILOSOPHE LES VERMELLES

June continued ②

taking over from the 19th London Regt & forming part of the Brigade Reserve for X Section of the Defences.

1 Rfn accidentally wounded by a bomb.

13th Bn remained Le PHILOSOPHE

14th do do.

2nd Lt WA Brooke was killed & Lt GN Clarke wounded while with the Bn Machine Section at X1 Section.

15. Bn remained LE PHILOSOPHE.

Lt Whelan RAMC joined from England for duty

16. The Bn took over X1 Section of the line from the 6th Bn London Regt.

Nos 1. 2. 4 Coys were in the Firing Line & No 3 Coy in Bn Reserve. Lt Falconer RAMC to England.

17, 18, 19, 20, 21 } The Bn occupied the Trenches taken over

22nd The Bn was relieved by the 6th Bn London Regt & returned to its former billets at Le PHILOSOPHE.

June continued (3)

June 23 }
    24 } The Bn remained at LE PHILOSOPHE
    25 } Capt Alexander rejoined for duty. —"—
    26 } —"—
    27 Bn remained at LE PHILOSOPHE
notification was received that the following had been awarded the DCM
No 474 Coy Sgt Major Peat
No 1473 a/Sgt W G Heather
No 2102 —"— F C Morel
No 64 a/c G H Mills RAMC attached

" 28th The Bn was lent to the 141st Bde the remaining Bns going into Bde Reserve.
2 Coys & Headquarters moved to MAZINGARBE the remainder remaining at PHILOSOPHE taking over billets from the 15th Bn
1 Rfn killed & 2 wounded

29. Bn remained in Reserve to 141st Bde at MAZINGARBE & PHILOSOPHE.

30. do do 1 Rfn accidently wounded

June continued (4) 72

Casualties to end of June

	Officers	Other Ranks
Killed	5	58
Wounded	9	306
Died of Wounds	3	11
Missing	-	-

Enclosed with June Diary,

1. Operation Orders 140th Inf Bde 9 – 17 both inclusive x

2. Maps of FESTHUBERT – GIVENCHY – LA BASSEE – VERMELLES marked into Sections

[signature]
Capt & Adj.

SECRET. COPY No. 5

OPERATION ORDER No.10

by

Brigadier General G.J.Cuthbert, C.B.,

Commanding 140th Infantry Brigade.

6th June, 1915.

1. On the night of 7th-8th June
   (a) The 7th Bn.London Regiment in Y.1 Section will be relieved by the 1st Bn.King's Royal Rifle Corps using boyau 80 and 81 for the purpose.
   (b) The 8th Bn.London Regiment in Y.2 Section will be relieved by the 1st Bn.South Staffordshire Regiment using boyau 83 and 8 for the purpose.

2. The Officers Commanding the 7th and 8th Battalions will send guides to meet their relieving Battalions to be outside the Brewery at VERMELLES at 8.30 p.m. to await the arrival of relieving Units.
   The South Staffords will arrive first, followed by the King's Royal Rifles.

3. The completion of reliefs will be reported at once to Brigade Headquarters.

4. All trench stores, including S.A.A. and bombs, will be handed over to the relieving Battalions and receipts obtained for them. Battalions will take away their own tools.

5. The relief of the Machine Guns in the Sections will be carried out as arranged between Brigade Machine Gun Officers.

6. No troops will move until after the arrival of the relieving troops, and no move will commence before 8.30 p.m.

7. On completion of reliefs, the 7th Bn.London Regiment will march independently into billets at MAZINGARBE, and the 8th Bn. London Regiment into NOEUX-LES-MINES.

8. The 15th Bn.London Regiment will, on relief by a battalion of the 6th Infantry Brigade, move into billets ~~into billets~~ at LES BREBIS, and will come under orders of the G.O.C. 142nd Infantry Brigade.

9. The 6th Bn.London Regiment will, on relief by a battalion of the 6th Infantry Brigade, move into billets at MAZINGARBE.

10. All transport, except cookers, will move to and be billeted at NOEUX LES MINES. Transport Officers will meet the Staff Captain at the Church at NOEUX LES MINES at 11.30 a.m. tomorrow.

11. Trench Mortars and personnel will be at NOEUX-LES-MINES and will be attached to the 8th Bn.London Regiment.

12. After relief, the 140th Infantry Brigade (less 15th Bn.London Regiment) will form the Divisional Reserve.

13. Billeting parties of 6th and 7th Battalions to meet the Staff Captain at 10 a.m. tomorrow at the Church at MAZINGARBE, and the 8th Battalion at NOEUX-LES-MINES at 11 a.m. The Billeting Officer of the 15th Bn.London Regiment will report to Headquarters, 142nd

23

Infantry Brigade, for instructions as to billeting in LES BREBIS.

14. There will be a Collecting Station at CHATEAU MAZINGARBE (L.23.b).

15. Brigade Headquarters will, on completion of the relief, move to MAZINGARBE.

R. Tempest Major,
Brigade Major,
140th Infantry Brigade.

Issued typewritten at 9.45 p.m.

Copy No. 1 - War Diary.
,, 2 - Operation Order File.
,, 3 - O.C.6th Bn.Lon.Regt. By Signal Service.
,, 4 - O.C.7th Bn. ,, ,,
,, 5 - O.C.8th Bn. ,, ,,
,, 6 - O.C.15th Bn. ,, ,,
,, 7 - G.O.C.142nd Inf.Bde. (for information) ,,
,, 8 - G.O.C. 6th Inf.Bde. (for information) ,,

"A" Form.

Army Form C. 2121.

MESSAGES AND SIGNALS.

No. of Message

Prefix Code m. Words Charge

Office of Origin and Service Instructions.

Sent At m. To By

This message is on a/c of: Service.

(Signature of "Franking Officer")

Recd. at m. Date From By

TO Eighth Lon Regt

Sender's Number	Day of Month	In reply to Number	AAA
BM 122	12.		

Reference	Operation	ordr	No 11	para
4	for	L 17 c	read	G.13.a.
AAA	Acknowledge	AAA		

From 140 Lon Inf Bde

Place

Time 5:30 pm

The above may be forwarded as now corrected. (Z)

Censor. Signature of Addressor or person authorised to telegraph in his name R Tempest Major

* This line should be erased if not required

C27642 P.G. Ltd. Wt. W14142/641—20,000 3/15 Forms C2121/10

25

SECRET.

Copy No.......

OPERATION ORDERS No.11
by
Brigadier General G.J.Cuthbert, C.B.,
Commanding 140th Infantry Bde.

19

12th June, 1915.

1. The 140th Infantry Brigade will relieve the 141st Infantry Brigade in X Section on the night of 12th/13th June.

2. The 6th Battalion will relieve the 20th Battalion in X1. Guides from the 20th Battalion will meet the Battalion at HALTE (G.20.A) at ~~[illegible]~~ 4.0p.m. today. Reliefs will be carried out by platoons at 3 minute intervals.

3. The 7th Battalion will relieve the 17th Battalion in X2 Section. Guides from the 17th Battalion will meet the Battalion at HALTE (G.20.A) at 8.0p.m. The relief will be carried out by platoons at 3 minute intervals.

4. The 8th Battalion will relieve the 19th Battalion in billets at PHILOSOPHE - L.17.c. This Battalion will not leave NOEUX LES MINES before 8.45 p.m. Billeting parties will be sent forward before the arrival of the Battalion to take over the billets.

5. Completion of reliefs will be reported to Brigade Headquarters.

6. Trench stores will be taken over.

7. The relief of the machine guns in the section will be carried out as arranged between Brigade Machine Gun Officers.

8. Transport will not be moved.

9. Brigade Headquarters will move to LE SAULCHOY Farm - L.17.d at 9,0p.m.

R. Tempest.
Major,
Brigade Major,
140th Infantry Brigade.

Issued typewritten at 12.0 Noon

Copy No.1 War Diary.
,, 2 Operation Order File.
,, 3 O.C.,6th Battn.Lond.Regt. By Signal Section.
,, 4 O.C.,7th ,, ,,
,, 5 O.C.,8th ,, ,,
,, 6 G.O.C.,141st Infantry Brigade. ,,
(for information).
,, 7 O.C.,15th Battn.Lond.Regt. ,,
(for information)

Copy No. 5

SECRET.

OPERATION ORDERS NO.12

140th Infantry Brigade.

20

June 15th, 1915.

1. The 8th Battalion The London Regiment (Post Office Rifles) will relieve the 6th Battalion The London Regiment on June 16th 1915.

2. Guides from the 6th Battalion will meet the 8th Battalion at the 6th Battalion Headquarters at 4.0p.m. June 16th, 1915. Reliefs will be carried out by platoon at, at least, 3 minutes interval.

3. Completion of reliefs will be reported to Brigade Headquarters.

4. Trench stores will be taken over, receipts given and a copy sent to Brigade Headquarters by the 8th Battalion.

Edward Oswald [signature]

Captain,
for Brigade Major,
140th Infantry Brigade.

Issued typewritten at 2.30p.m.

Copy No.1 ... War Diary
,, 2 ... Operation Order File.
,, 3 ... O.C.,6th Battalion London Regt, By Signal Sect.
,, 4 ... O.C.,7th ,, ,, ,,
,, 5 ... O.C.,8th ,, ,, ,,

SECRET.

No. 5.

OPERATION ORDER NO.15

by

Brigadier General G.J Cuthbert, C.B.,

Commanding 140th Infantry Brigade.

20th June, 1915.

1. The 15th Bn., The London Regiment (Civil Service Rifles) will relieve the 7th Battalion, The London Regiment, on June 21st, 1915.

2. Guides from the 7th Battalion will meet the 15th Battalion at the 7th Battalion Headquarters at 6.30 p.m. June 21st, 1915. Reliefs will be carried out by platoons. Officers of the 15th Battalion will reconnoitre the line by daylight before taking over.

3. Completion of relief will be reported to Brigade Headquarters.

4. Trench Stores will be taken over, receipts given, and a copy sent to Brigade Headquarters by 7th Battalion.

5. The 7th Battalion will take over the billets of the 15th Battalion under arrangements to be made between Officers Commanding Battalions.

[illegible signature]
Captain,
for Brigade Major,
140th Infantry Brigade.

Issued typewritten at 4 p.m.

Copy No. 1	Operation Order File.		
,, 2	War Diary.		
,, 3	6th Bn.London Regt.		By Signal Section.
,, 4	7th	,,	,,
,, 5	8th	,,	,,
,, 6	15th	,,	,,

28

Copy No....5....

SECRET.

OPERATION ORDER NO.14

140th Infantry Brigade.

22

21st June,1915.

1. The 6th Battalion London Regiment will relieve the 8th Battalion London Regiment on June 22nd,1915.

2. Guides from the 8th Battalion will meet the 6th Battalion at the 8th Battalion Headquarters at 8,30p.m.,June 22nd,1915. Reliefs will be carried out by platoons.

3. Completion of relief will be reported to Brigade Headquarters.

4. Trench Stores will be taken over, receipts given, and a copy sent to Brigade Headquarters by the 6th Battalion.

5. The 8th Battalion will take over the billets of the 6th Battalion under arrangements to be made between Officers Commanding Battalions.

Edward Vassilen
Captain,
for Brigade Major,
140th Infantry Brigade.

Issued typewritten at 8.45p.m.

Copy No.1	Operation Order File.		
,, 2	War Diary.		
,, 3	6th Battalion London Regiment, by Signals.		
,, 4	7th ,,	,,	,,
,, 5	8th ,,	,,	,,
,, 6	15th ,,	,,	,,

282

29

SECRET.

COPY No. 5.

OPERATION ORDER No. 15.

140th Infantry Brigade.

23

25th June, 1915.

1. The 7th Battalion, The London Regiment, will relieve the 15th Battalion, The London Regiment (Civil Service Rifles), in X.2 on June 26th, 1915.

2. Guides from the 15th Battalion will meet the 7th Battalion at the Western end of Trench 12 at 8.30 p.m., June 26th, 1915. Reliefs will be carried out by platoons.

3. The completion of the relief will be reported to Brigade Headquarters.

4. Trench Stores will be taken over, receipts given, and a copy sent to Brigade Headquarters by 15th Battalion.
Periscopes and Very Pistols will not be handed over.

5. The 15th Battalion will take over the billets at present occupied by the 7th Battalion, under arrangements to be made between Officers Commanding Battalions.

[illegible]
Captain,
for Brigade Major,
140th Infantry Brigade.

Issued typewritten at 11 a.m.

Copy No. 1	...	War Diary.	
,, 2	...	Operation Order File.	
,, 3	...	O.C.6th Bn.Lon.Regt.	By Signal Section.
,, 4	...	O.C.7th do.	do.
,, 5	...	O.C.8th do.	do.
,, 6	...	O.C.15th do.	do.
,, 7	...	G.O.C.5th Inf.Bde. (for information).	do.

30

"A" Form. Army Form C. 2121.

MESSAGES AND SIGNALS. No. of Message

Prefix Code m.	Words 17	Charge	This message is on a/c of:	Recd. at m.
Office of Origin and Service Instructions. 23D	Sent At m. To By		Service. (Signature of "Franking Officer.")	Date 27/6/15 From By

TO 8TH LON REGT

Sender's Number	Day of Month	In reply to Number	AAA
*BM/786B	Twentyseven		

Operating order no 16 Cancelled aaa

From 140 TH INF BDE 8 AM
Place
Time

The above may be forwarded as now corrected. (Z)

Censor. Signature of Addressor or person authorised to telegraph in his name.

* This line should be erased if not required.

292116—W. & S. Ltd., London—W 11142 641—20,000—4/15. Forms C 2121/10.

PUBLIC RECORD
OFFICE

SECRET.

COPY No. 5

OPERATION ORDER No. 16.

140th Infantry Brigade.

26th June, 1915.

1. The 8th Battalion, The London Regiment (Post Office Rifles) will relieve the 6th Battalion, The London Regiment (Rifles), in X.1 on June 27th, 1915.

2. Guides from the 6th Battalion will meet the 8th Battalion at the ~~Western end of Trench 12~~ 6th Bn Headquarters at 8.30 p.m., June 27th, 1915. Reliefs will be carried out by platoons.

3. The completion of the relief will be reported to Brigade Headquarters.

4. Trench Stores will be taken over, receipts given, and a copy sent to Brigade Headquarters by the 8th Battalion.

Periscopes and Very pistols will not be handed over.

5. The 6th Battalion will take over the billets at present occupied by the 8th Battalion, under arrangements to be made between Officers Commanding Battalions.

Edward Chandler
Captain,
for Brigade Major,
140th Infantry Brigade.

Issued typewritten at 4 p.m.

Copy No. 1	...	War Diary.		
,, 2	...	Operation Order File.		
,, 3	...	O.C. 6th Bn.Lon.Regt.	By Signal Section.	
,, 4	...	O.C. 7th do.	do.	
,, 5	...	O.C. 8th do.	do.	
,, 6	...	O.C.15th do.	do.	
,, 7	...	G.O.C.141st Inf.Bde. (for information).	do.	

Copy No..5....

SECRET. OPERATION ORDERS NO.17

140th Infantry Bde.

27th June,1916.

1. The 140th Infantry Brigade will be relieved by the 142nd Infantry Brigade, in Section X, on the night of June 28th,1916.

2. The 8th Battalion London Regiment in X1 will be relieved by the 22nd Battalion London Regiment. Company Officers of the 22nd Battalion will reconnoitre the line by daylight and will be met by guides of the 8th Battalion at the western end of Trench 12 at 5.0p.m. Guides of the 8th Battalion will meet the 22nd Battn. at western end of Trench 12 at 9.30p.m.
On relief, the 8th Battalion will take over the billets of the 22nd Battalion at MAZINGARBE. Billeting party to be at the Church at MAZINGARBE at 5.0p.m.

3. The 7th Battalion London Regiment will be relieved by the 23rd and 24th Battalions,London Regiment in X2. Company Officers of 23rd and 24th Battalions will reconnoitre the line by daylight and will be met by guides of the 7th Battalion at the western end of Trench 12 at 5.0p.m. Guides of the 7th Battalion will meet the 23rd and 24th Battalions at the western end of Trench 12 at 9.30p.m. On relief, the 7th Battalion will take over the billets of the 21st Battalion London Regiment at MAZINGARBE. Billeting party to be at the Church at MAZINGARBE at 5.0p.m.

4. The 21st Battalion will take over the billets of the 6th Battalion at LE PHILOSOPHE. The billeting party of the 21st Battalion will be at the 6th Battalion Headquarters at 5.0p.m. The 6th Battalion will be clear of their billets by 8.0p.m. The 6th Battalion will take over the billets of the 15th Battalion at LE PHILOSOPHE and MAZINGARBE,under arrangements to be made between O.C.Battalions, and will come under the command of the G.O.C., 142nd Infantry Brigade. It will not take over a section of the trenches whilst so attached. The two Companies of the 6th Battn. to be billeted at MAZINGARBE will march to their billets by platoons.

5. The 15th Battalion London Regiment will take over the billets of the 23rd and 24th Battalions,London Regiment at NOEUX LES MINES, leaving their present billets at 8.0p.m. and marching by platoons.
Billeting parties will be at the Church at NOEUX LES MINES at 5.0p.m.

6. All trench stores will be handed over, including VERMOREL Sprayers, and receipts sent to this office. Periscopes and VERY Pistols will not be handed over. A list of trench stores to be handed over will be sent to the Brigade Office by 5.0p.m., June 28th,1916.

7. The transport of Battalions will remain in its present situations.

8. Battalions will report relief to Brigade Headquarters immediately on completion.

9. Brigade Headquarters will move to NOEUX LES MINES (R.18.b) on completion of reliefs.

10.The

33

10. The 6th London Field Ambulance is situated at NOEUX LES MINES.

Captain,
for Brigade Major,
140th Infantry Brigade.

Issued typewritten at 4.0p.m.

Copy No.1	...	War Diary.	
,, 2	...	Operation Order File.	
,, 3	...	O.C.6th Bn.Lond.Regt.	By Signal Service.
,, 4	...	O.C.7th ,,	,,
,, 5	...	O.C.8th ,,	,,
,, 6	...	O.C.15th ,,	,,
,, 7	...	G.O.C.,142nd Infantry Bde. (for information)	,,

33
34

Copy No. 5

Operation Orders No.2.
by
Brigadier General G.J.Cuthbert, C. B.,
Commanding 140th Infantry Bde.

18

1st June,1915.

Ref.Map BETHUNE, 1/40000.

1. During the night of 1/2 June the 140th Infantry Brigade will take over Y1 and Y2 Sections of the VERMELLES line.

2. a. Y1 Section will be taken over by the 7th Battn.Lond.Regt. who will relieve the 1st Battalion Coldstream Guards.
The 7th Battn.Lond.Regt.will march from its billets independently and will pass SAILLY LA BOURSE at 8.30p.m.tonight.
Guides will meet the Battalion at Cross Roads L11c2.5 and will take the Battalion by the SAILLY-LENS road, cross roads G13d, Cross roads G8 a c.

b. Y2 Section will be taken over by the 8th Battn.Lond.Regt. who will relieve the London Scottish.
The 8th Battalion London Regt.will march from its billets independently and will pass SAILLY LA BOURSE immediately in rear of the 7th Battalion London Regt.
Guides will meet the Battalion at the cross roads L 11c2.5 and will take the Battalion by road L 11b and the road L 12a not marked on the map.

Machines Guns.

c. Y1. 3 guns in the front line and 1 at LE RUTOIRE will be relieved by 2 guns of the 7th Battalion and 2 guns of the 15th Battalion. Guides will be at the same places as Company guides.
Y2. 2 guns of the London Scottish, 1 of Black Watch, and 1 gun of Scots Guards in the second line HULLUCH road will be relieved by 2 guns of the 8th Battalion and 2 guns of the 6th Battalion. The Machine Gun Officer,London Scottish is arranging guides.

d.Battalions will report when they have taken over and the usual situation and progress reports will be rendered.

3. Battalions will take their own Battalion tools into the trenches. Bombs will be found in the trenches with the trench stores.

4. The 6th (leading Battalion) and 15th Battalions will leave BETHUNE at 8p.m. and march via BEUVRY and move into billets as follows:- 6th Battn. NOYELLES LEZ VERMELLES.
15th Battn. SAILLY-LA-BOURSE,
and will come into Brigade Reserve.

5. Captain Gaze, 15th Battalion, will take over the Brigade Reserve S.A.A.including the 200 bombs on charge from the 1st Battalion Scots Guards.

6. Owing to the new area being in sight of the enemy's observation stations, troops will not move by day in larger formations than a platoon or 4 vehicles.
Transport, except in case of emergency will not move East of a N.and S. line through VERQUIN before 7.30p.m.

7. The 4th London Field Company R.E.will move from GORRE into billets at SAILLY LA BOURSE and will march via BEUVRY. They will pass BEUVRY Church at 8.55p.m. and will follow in rear of the 15th Battalion London Regt.

2.

35

8. The 4th London Field Ambulance will have a detachment at SAILLY LA BOURSE. Train will be at HESDIGNEUL.

9. Refilling point for June 2nd HESDIGNEUL at 11 a.m.

10. Brigade Office closes at BETHUNE 5p.m. and reopens at NOYELLES LEZ VERMELLES at 6p.m.

R. Temperet. Major,
Brigade Major,
140th Infantry Brigade.

Issued typewritten at 5.30p.m.

Copy No.	1	War Diary	
,,	2	Operation Order File	
,,	3	O.C. 6th Battalion London Regt.	By Signal Service.
,,	4	O.C. 7th do.	,,
,,	5	O.C. 8th do.	,,
,,	6	O.C.15th do.	,,
,,	7	O.C.,4th Lon.Field Co.R.E.	,,
,,	8	G.O.C.1st Guards Brigade for information.	,,

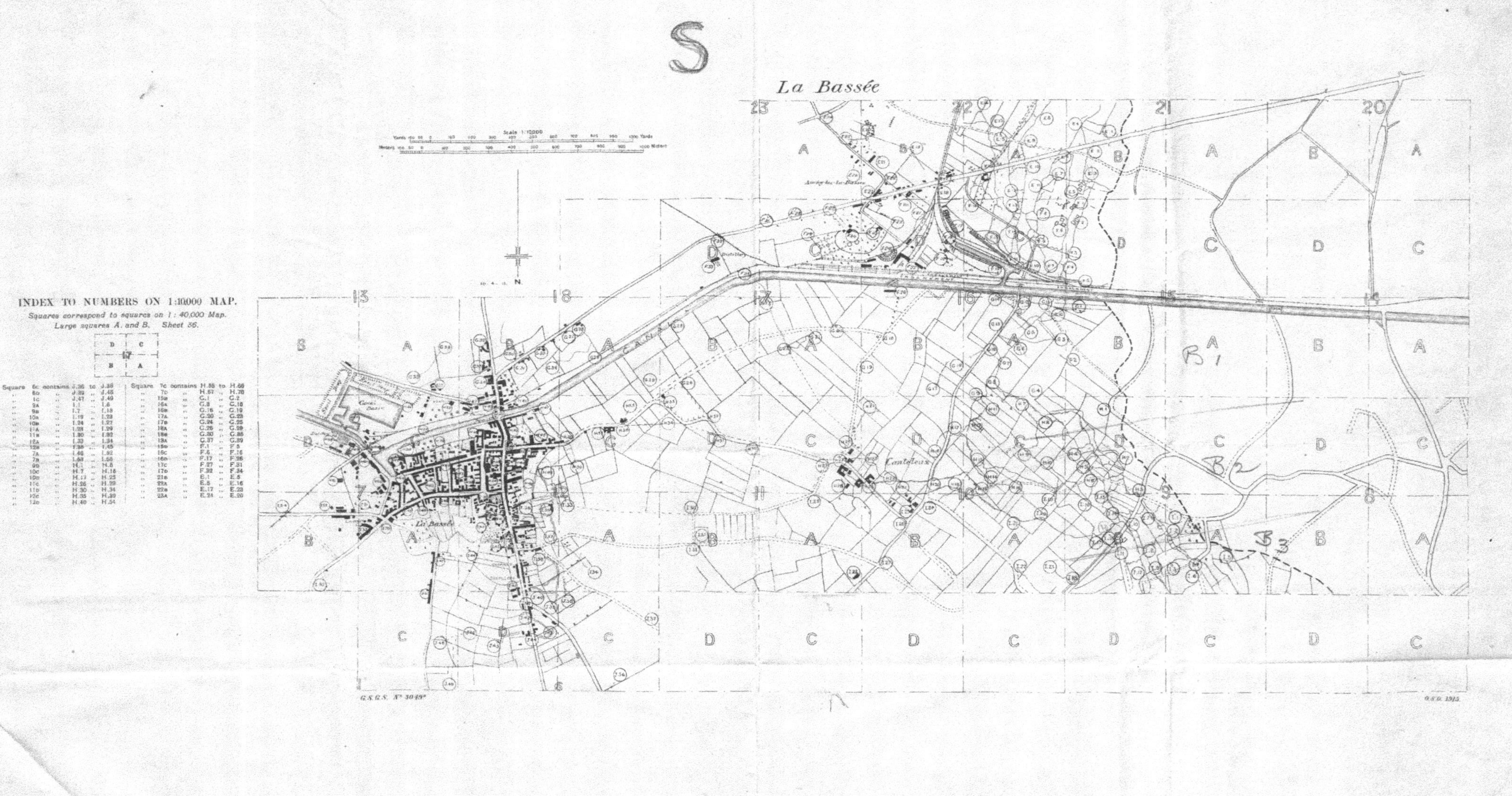

S
La Bassée
Scale 1:10,000
Yards
Meters
N
CANAL
Canteleux
La Bassée
INDEX TO NUMBERS ON 1:10,000 MAP.
Squares correspond to squares on 1 : 40,000 Map.
Large squares A. and B. Sheet 36.
D C
17
B A
Square 6C contains J.36 to J.38
" 6D " J.39 " J.46
" 1C " J.47 " J.49
" 9A " I.1 " I.6
" 9B " I.7 " I.18
" 10A " I.19 " I.23
" 10B " I.24 " I.27
" 11A " I.28 " I.29
" 11B " I.30 " I.32
" 12A " I.33 " I.34
" 12B " I.35 " I.45
" 7A " I.46 " I.52
" 7B " I.53 " I.56
" 9D " H.1 " H.6
" 10C " H.7 " H.16
" 10D " H.17 " H.25
" 11C " H.26 " H.29
" 11D " H.30 " H.34
" 12C " H.35 " H.39
" 12D " H.40 " H.54
Square 7C contains H.55 to H.66
" 7D " H.67 " H.70
" 15B " G.1 " G.2
" 16A " G.3 " G.15
" 16B " G.16 " G.19
" 17A " G.20 " G.23
" 17B " G.24 " G.25
" 18A " G.26 " G.29
" 18B " G.30 " G.36
" 13A " G.37 " G.39
" 15D " F.1 " F.5
" 16C " F.6 " F.16
" 16D " F.17 " F.26
" 17C " F.27 " F.31
" 17D " F.32 " F.34
" 21B " E.1 " E.5
" 22A " E.5 " E.16
" 22B " E.17 " E.23
" 23A " E.24 " E.30

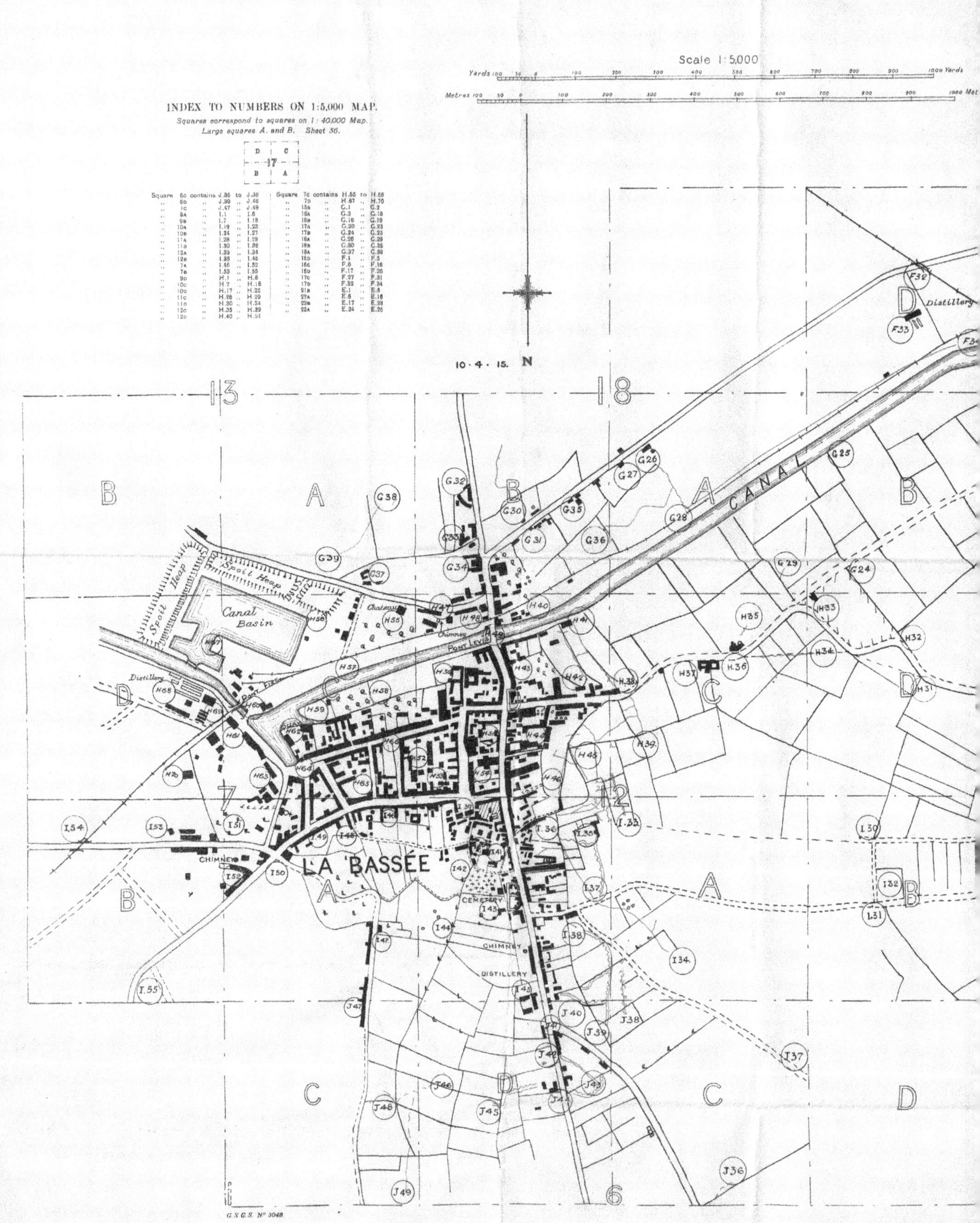

INDEX TO NUMBERS ON 1:5,000 MAP.

Squares correspond to squares on 1 : 40,000 Map.
Large squares A. and B. Sheet 36.

D	C
B	A

(17)

Square		contains		to		Square		contains		to	
Square	6c	contains	J.36	to	J.38	Square	7c	contains	H.55	to	H.66
,,	6D	,,	J.39	,,	J.46	,,	7D	,,	H.67	,,	H.70
,,	1c	,,	J.47	,,	J.49	,,	15B	,,	G.1	,,	G.2
,,	9A	,,	I.1	,,	I.6	,,	16A	,,	G.3	,,	G.15
,,	9B	,,	I.7	,,	I.18	,,	16B	,,	G.16	,,	G.19
,,	10A	,,	I.19	,,	I.23	,,	17A	,,	G.20	,,	G.23
,,	10B	,,	I.24	,,	I.27	,,	17B	,,	G.24	,,	G.25
,,	11A	,,	I.28	,,	I.29	,,	18A	,,	G.26	,,	G.29
,,	11B	,,	I.30	,,	I.32	,,	18B	,,	G.30	,,	G.36
,,	12A	,,	I.33	,,	I.34	,,	13A	,,	G.37	,,	G.39
,,	12B	,,	I.35	,,	I.45	,,	15D	,,	F.1	,,	F.5
,,	7A	,,	I.46	,,	I.52	,,	16C	,,	F.6	,,	F.16
,,	7B	,,	I.53	,,	I.55	,,	16D	,,	F.17	,,	F.26
,,	9D	,,	H.1	,,	H.6	,,	17C	,,	F.27	,,	F.31
,,	10C	,,	H.7	,,	H.16	,,	17D	,,	F.32	,,	F.34
,,	10D	,,	H.17	,,	H.25	,,	21B	,,	E.1	,,	E.5
,,	11C	,,	H.26	,,	H.29	,,	22A	,,	E.6	,,	E.16
,,	11D	,,	H.30	,,	H.34	,,	22B	,,	E.17	,,	E.23
,,	12C	,,	H.35	,,	H.39	,,	23A	,,	E.24	,,	E.26
,,	12D	,,	H.40	,,	H.54						

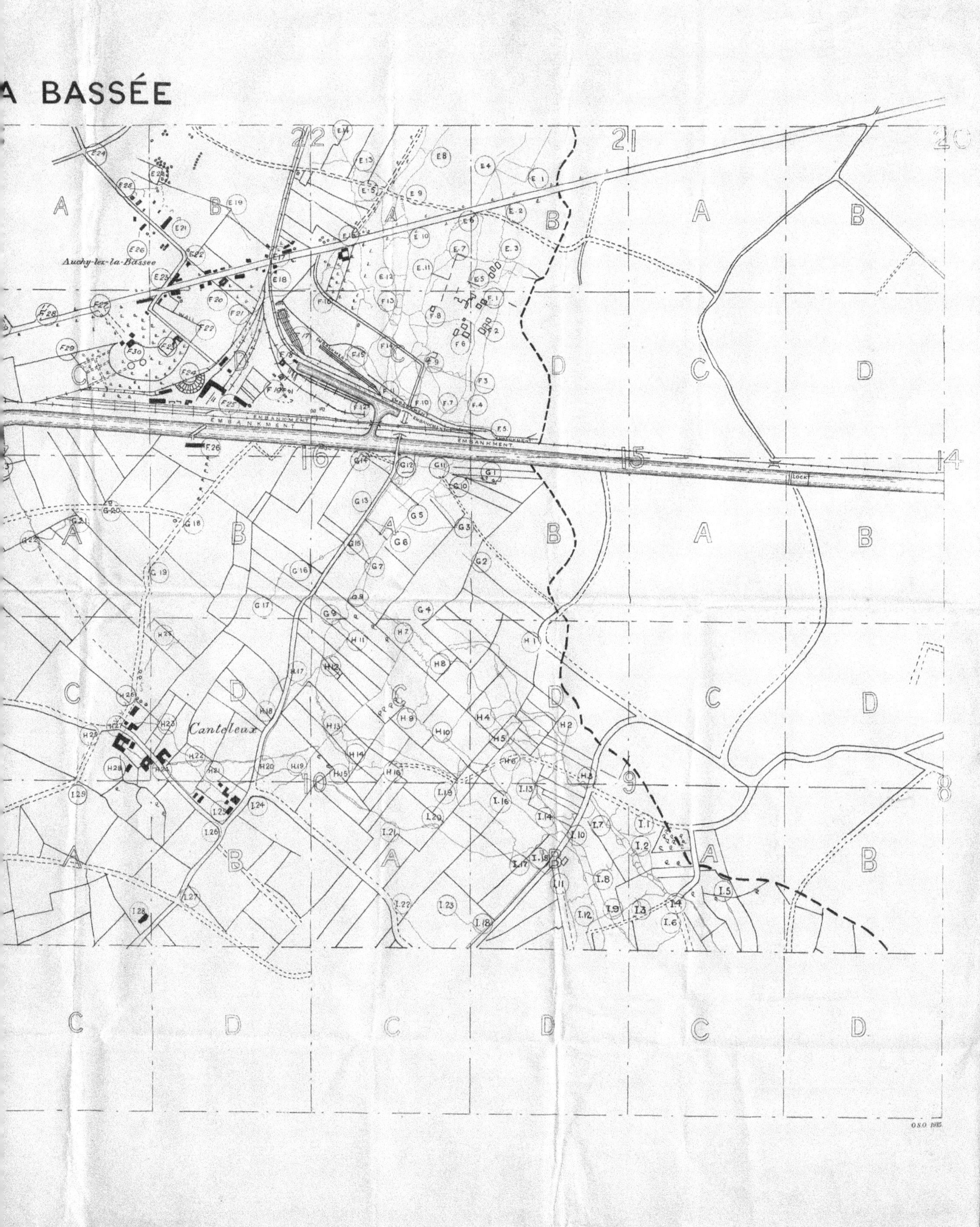

A BASSÉE
Auchy-lez-la-Bassée
Canteleux
EMBANKMENT
LOCK
WALL
O.S.O. 1915

LA BASSE $\frac{1}{5000}$

ILLIES, VIOLAINE

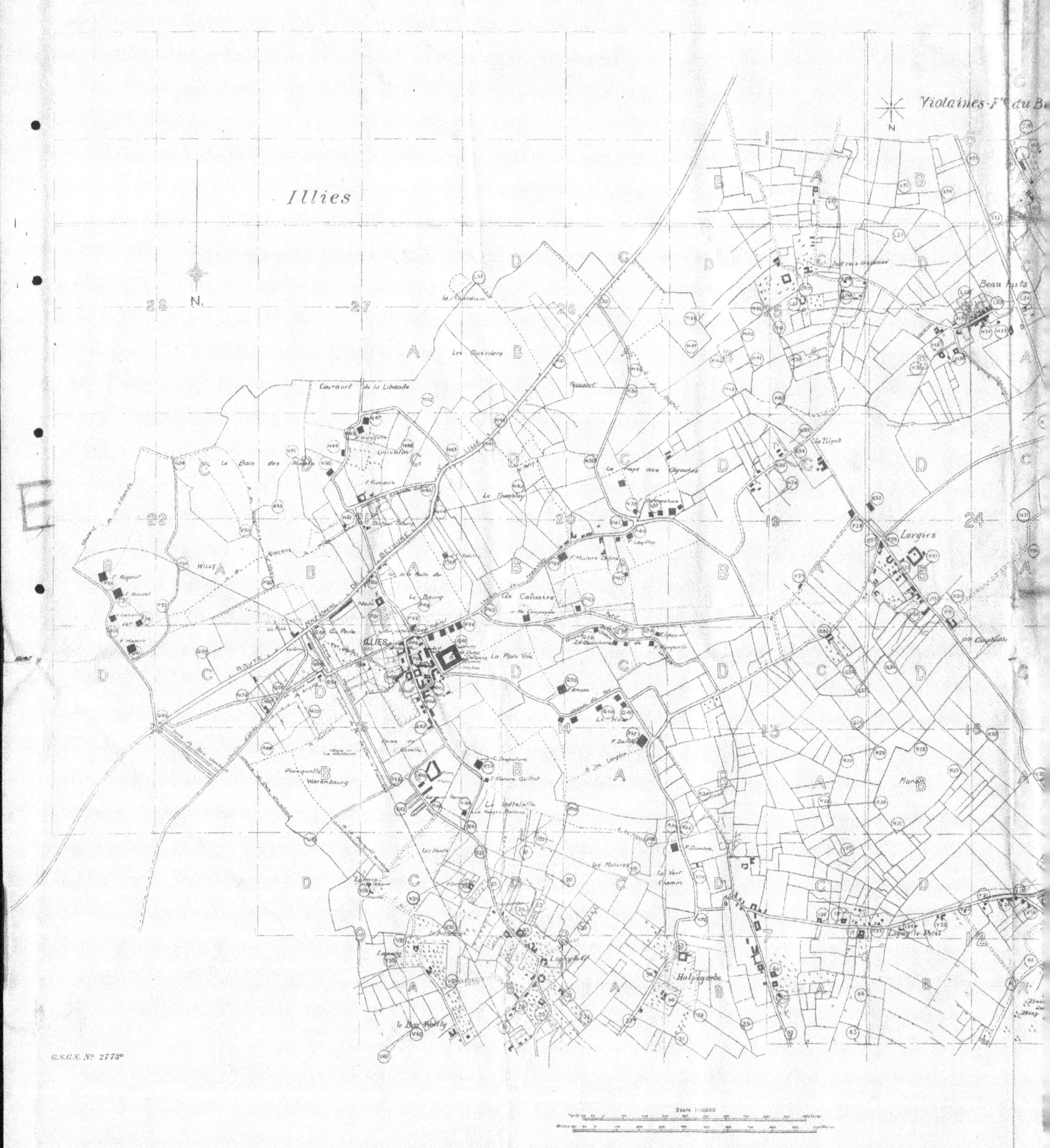

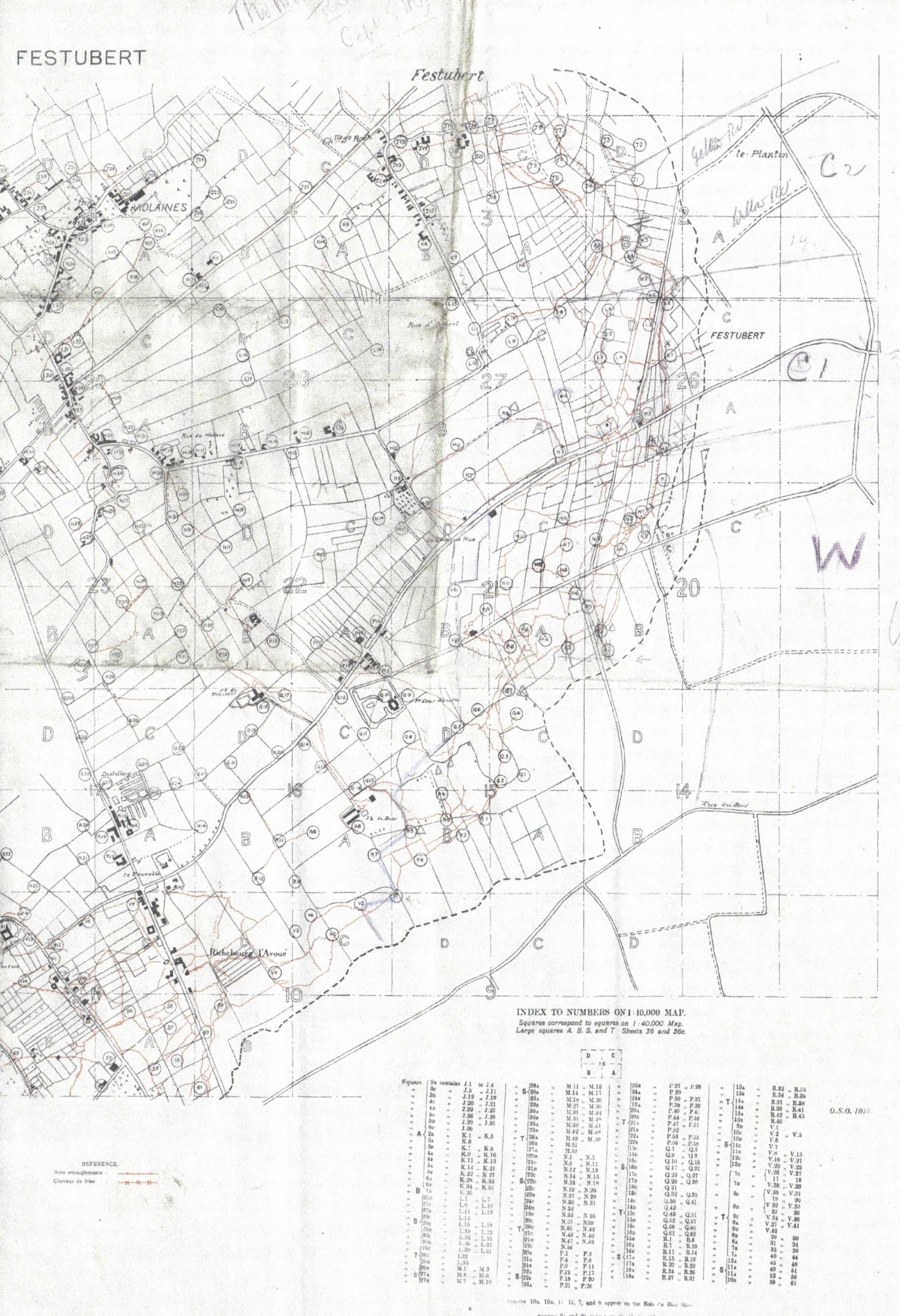

INDEX TO NUMBERS ON 1:10,000 MAP.

Squares correspond to squares on 1:40,000 Map.
Large squares A. B. S. and T Sheets 36 and 36c.

Large square	Square	Contains
A	2D	J.1 to J.4
A	3C	J.5 to J.11
A	3D	J.12 to J.19
A	4C	J.20 to J.21
A	4D	J.22 to J.25
A	5C	J.26 to J.28
A	5D	J.29 to J.35
A	6C	J.36
A	2B	K.1 to K.5
A	3A	K.6
A	3B	K.7 to K.8
A	4A	K.9 to K.10
A	4B	K.11 to K.13
A	5A	K.14 to K.21
A	5B	K.22 to K.27
A	6A	K.28 to K.33
A	6B	K.34 to K.35
B	1A	K.36
S	26D	L.1 to L.7
S	27C	L.8 to L.10
S	27D	L.11 to L.13
S	28C	L.14
S	28D	L.15 to L.18
S	29D	L.19 to L.23
S	30C	L.24 to L.25
S	30D	L.26 to L.27
T	25C	L.28 to L.31
T	26C	L.32
T	26D	L.33
T	26B	M.1 to M.3
S	27A	M.4 to M.6
S	27B	M.7 to M.10
S	28A	M.11 to M.13
S	28B	M.14 to M.17
S	29A	M.18 to M.26
S	29B	M.27 to M.30
S	30A	M.31 to M.34
S	30B	M.35 to M.38
T	25A	M.39 to M.41
T	25B	M.42 to M.48
T	26A	M.49 to M.50
T	26B	M.51
T	27A	M.52
S	20D	N.1 to N.5
S	21C	N.6 to N.11
S	21D	N.12 to N.13
S	22C	N.14 to N.15
S	22D	N.16 to N.18
S	23C	N.19 to N.26
S	23D	N.27 to N.29
S	24C	N.30 to N.31
S	24D	N.32
T	19C	N.33 to N.36
T	20C	N.37 to N.39
T	20D	N.40 to N.42
T	21C	N.43 to N.46
T	21D	N.47 to N.53
T	22C	N.54
S	20B	P.1 to P.3
S	21A	P.4 to P.8
S	21B	P.9 to P.11
S	22A	P.12 to P.17
S	22B	P.18 to P.20
S	23A	P.21 to P.26
	23B	P.27 to P.28
	24A	P.29
	24B	P.30 to P.37
T	19A	P.38 to P.39
T	20A	P.40 to P.43
T	20B	P.44 to P.46
T	21A	P.47 to P.51
T	21B	P.52
T	22A	P.53 to P.55
T	22B	P.56 to P.58
S	15C	Q.1 to Q.5
S	15D	Q.6 to Q.9
S	16C	Q.10 to Q.16
S	16D	Q.17 to Q.22
S	17C	Q.23 to Q.27
S	17D	Q.28 to Q.30
S	18C	Q.31
T	13C	Q.32 to Q.35
T	14C	Q.36 to Q.41
T	14D	Q.42
T	15C	Q.43 to Q.51
T	15D	Q.52 to Q.57
T	16C	Q.58 to Q.60
T	16D	Q.61 to Q.62
S	15B	R.1 to R.6
S	16A	R.7 to R.10
S	16B	R.11 to R.14
S	17A	R.15 to R.19
S	17B	R.20 to R.23
S	18A	R.24 to R.26
S	18B	R.27 to R.31
T	13A	R.32 to R.33
T	13B	R.34 to R.36
T	14A	R.37 to R.38
T	14B	R.39 to R.41
T	15A	R.42 to R.45
T	15B	R.46
S	9D	V.1
S	10C	V.2 to V.5
S	10D	V.6
S	11C	V.7
S	11D	V.8 to V.15
S	12C	V.16 to V.21
S	12D	V.22 to V.25
T	7C	V.26 to V.27; 17 to 18
T	7D	V.28 to V.29
T	8C	V.30 to V.31; 19 to 20
T	8D	V.32 to V.33; 22 to 26
T	9C	V.34 to V.36
T	9A	V.37 to V.41
T	9D	V.42
T	8B	28 to 30
T	8A	31 to 34
T	7B	35 to 39
T	7A	40 to 44
S	12A	45 to 48
S	11B	49 to 51
S	11A	52 to 58
S	10B	59 to 61

Squares 10A, 10B, 11, 12, 7, and 8 appear on the Bois de Biez Sheet.

Squares 9A and 9C appear on the Herlies Sheet.

140th Bde.

47th Div.

1/8th LONDON REGT.

JULY

1 9 1 5

Attached:
140th Inf. Bde. O. Os.
Nos. 18, 19, 20 and 21.
142nd Inf Bde O.Os
Nos. 24 and 25.

On His Majesty's Service.

40

10

47th Division

121/6539

8th London Regt.

Vol V

From 1st to 31st July 1915

Nil

41

SECRET.   Copy No. 5

OPERATION ORDERS NO.18

140th Infantry Brigade.

1st July, 1915.

1. The 15th Battalion London Regiment (Civil Service Rifles) will move into billets at MAZINGARBE on the night of July 1st, 1915.

2. Headquarters and 2 Companies of the 15th Battalion will take over the billets now occupied by the Headquarters and 2 Companies of the 8th Battalion. The billets of the remaining 2 Companies will be notified later.

3. On receipt of orders for Bde to move ~~No move will take place before 8.30p.m.~~ Bde H.Q. moves to Chateau Mazingarbe [illegible] as before

4. The arrival of the Battalion at MAZINGARBE will be reported to Brigade Headquarters.

5. Transport will remain in its present situation except cookers and water carts.

Edward [illegible]
Captain,
for Brigade Major,
140th Infantry Brigade.

Issued typewritten at 11.0 a.m.

Copy No.1	War Diary,		
,, 2	Operation Order File,		
,, 3	O.C., 6th Battalion Lond.Regt.		By Signal Service
,, 4	O.C., 7th	,,	,,
,, 5	O.C., 8th	,,	,,
,, 6	O.C., 15th	,,	,,

42

SECRET. Copy No. 9.

OPERATION ORDER No. 19.

140th Infantry Brigade.

1. The 140th Infantry Brigade will relieve the 141st Infantry Brigade in W Section on the night of July 6th-7th, 1915.

2. The 7th Bn. London Regiment will relieve the 20th Bn. London Regiment in W.1.
The 15th Bn. London Regiment will relieve the 18th Bn. London Regiment in W.2.
The 6th Bn. London Regiment will relieve the 19th Bn. London Regiment in W.3.
The 8th Bn. London Regiment will relieve the 17th Bn. London Regiment in Brigade Reserve, including the garrison of Keep C.

3. The 7th Battalion will be met by guides of the 20th Battn. at the Church at LES BREBIS at 9 p.m.
The 15th Battalion will be met by guides of the 18th Battn. at 18th Battalion Headquarters at 9.30 p.m.
The 6th Battalion will be met by guides of the 19th Battn. at LES BREBIS Church at 9.30 p.m.
The 8th Battalion will be met by guides of the 17th Battn. at the Church at LES BREBIS at 10 p.m.
Reliefs to take place by Platoons at 3 minutes intervals.

4. The Billeting Party and Reconnoitring Officer of the 8th Battalion will be met by guides of the 17th Battalion at LES BREBIS Church at 5 p.m.
The Billeting Party of the 20th Battalion will be met by guides of the 8th Battalion at the 8th Battalion Headquarters at LE PHILOSOPHE at 5 p.m.
The Billeting Parties of the 17th, 18th and 19th Battalions will be met respectively by guides of the 7th, 15th and 6th Battalions at the Church at MAZINGARBE at 5 p.m.

5. The relief of Machine Guns will be carried out under arrangements to be made by Brigade Machine Gun Officers of the 140th and 141st Infantry Brigades.

6. No. 3 Trench Mortar Battery will be attached for rations to the 15th Battalion from July 7th inclusive. The personnel consists of 1 Officer and 23 other ranks.

7. The Brigade Trench Mortar Battery will be formed under Lieut. CULVERWELL, 7th Battalion, who will make the necessary arrangements with Officers Commanding Battalions. It will be attached for rations to the 7th Battalion from July 8th inclusive.

8. Trench Stores (including VERMOREL SPRAYERS) will be taken over and receipts given.

9. A Brigade S.A.A. reserve, consisting of 2 S.A.A. wagons per battalion, will be formed on the road immediately N.E. of Brigade Headquarters at LES BREBIS, under arrangements to be made by Captain GAZE, 15th Battalion. The horses will return to their transport lines.

10. Battalion transport will remain in its present situations.

11. Brigade Headquarters will move from NOEUX LES MINES to LES BREBIS at 9.30 p.m.

43

12. Battalions will report relief to Brigade Headquarters at LES BREBIS immediately on completion.

13. The Dressing Station is situated at LES BREBIS.

14. Ration wagons will be brought up on July 6th so that rations may be issued before battalions move off. Wagons will move singly with at least 300 yards distance between wagons.

5th July, 1915.

Captain,
for Brigade Major,
140th Infantry Brigade.

NOTE.

It is notified for information that glanders and a particularly virulent form of mange are present among the French horses at LES BREBIS. The greatest care should therefore be taken when horses approach that neighbourhood, for however short a time, that they are not brought into contact with any French horses, or placed in buildings in which French horses have been stabled.

Issued typewritten at 7.45 p.m.

Copy No.			
1	...	War Diary.	
,, 2	...	Operation Order File.	
,, 3	...	G.O.C. 47th Division.	By Signal Section.
,, 4	...	G.O.C.141st Inf.Bde.	do.
,, 5	...	G.O.C.142nd Inf.Bde.	do.
,, 6	...	G.O.C.92nd French Div.	do.
,, 7	...	O.C. 6th Bn.Lon.Regt.	do.
,, 8	...	O.C. 7th ,,	do.
,, 9	...	O.C. 8th ,,	do.
,, 10	...	O.C.15th ,,	do.
,, 11	...	O.C.Bde.Ammn.Reserve.	do.
,, 12	...	O.C.Bde.Trench Mortar Battery.	do.

44

44

S E C R E T.

OPERATION ORDER NO.20

140th Infantry Brigade.

1. The 142nd Infantry Brigade will relieve the 140th Infantry Brigade in Section W on the night of the 22nd July.

2. On relief, the 140th Infantry Brigade less 7th Battalion London Regiment will go into Divisional Reserve.
The 7th Battalion will be placed at the disposal of the G.O.C. 142nd Infantry Brigade as Brigade Reserve. It will be billeted in SOUTH MAROC, and will not be available for duty in the trenches.

3. The 8th Battalion London Regt. will be relieved in W1 by the 21st Battalion.
The 15th Battalion London Regt. will be relieved in W2 by the 22nd Battalion.
The 6th Battalion London Regt. will be relieved in W3 by the 23rd and 24th Battalions.
The Battalions of the 142nd Infantry Brigade will leave MAZINGARBE at the following hours:-

21st Battalion at 8.30p.m.
22nd ,, 9. 0p.m.
23rd & 24th Battns. at 9.30p.m.

Further arrangements for the relief will be made between Officers Commanding Battalions concerned.

4. The 7th Battalion will take over the garrisoning of the keeps A,B,C and D from the 8th Battalion before dark.

5. The relief of the Machine Guns will be carried out under arrangements to be made between the Brigade Machine Gun Officers, 140th and 142nd Infantry Brigades.

6. No.8 Trench Mortar Battery will remain in W1 Section and will come under the command of the G.O.C., 142nd Infantry Brigade.

7. The 5 - 95mm. Trench Mortars in W1 will be handed over to the 142nd Infantry Brigade and the personnel will return to their units.

8. All trench stores will be handed over and receipts taken which will be forwarded to this office.
A list of all trench stores including bombs, ammunition, Vermorel Sprayers, etc. will be forwarded to this office by 2.0p.m., July 22nd.

9. On relief, the 8th Battalion will take over the billets of the 21st Battalion. Billeting Party to be at MAZINGARBE church at 5.0p.m.
The 6th Battalion will take over the billets of the 22nd Battalion. Billeting party to be at MAZINGARBE church at 5.15p.m.
The 15th Battalion will take over the billets of the 23rd and 24th Battalions. Billeting party to be at MAZINGARBE church at 5.30p.m.
The Companies of the 10th Gordon Highlanders and the 8th Seaforth Highlanders at present attached to the 7th and 15th Battalions respectively, will return to their billets after relief under arrangements to be made by Commanding Officers of their Units.
The parties of the 10th Scottish Rifles and the 12th Highland Light Infantry at present attached to the 7th and 15th Battalions respectively will be replaced at 7.0p.m. July 22nd by parties of the 8th Seaforth Highlanders and 10th Gordon Highlanders respectively. These parties will be met at Headquarters, 141st Infantry Brigade by guides of the 7th and 15th Battalions at 7.0p.m. and will remain in the Section after relief.

10.

45
PUBLIC RECORD

10. The Brigade Grenadier Company under Lieut.F.M.Davis, 7th Battalion London Regiment (less 7th Battalion Platoon) will be attached for billeting to the 8th Battalion. Each platoon will draw its rations from its own Battalion.

11. The waggons of Brigade Ammunition Reserve will rejoin their Units under instructions to be given by Captain Gaze, 15th Battn. London Regiment, no move to take place before 9.0 P,m.

12. Brigade Headquarters will close at LES BREBIS on completion of the reliefs and will open at NOEUX LES MINES on arrival there.

13. Transport of Battalions will remain in their present situations.

Edward Lascelles

Captain,
for Brigade Major,
140th Infantry Brigade.

Issued typewritten at 7.0p.m.

Copy No.	1	War Diary	
,,	2	Operation Order File.	
,,	3	G.O.C.,47th (London) Division.	By Signal Service.
,,	4	O.C.,6th Battn.Lond.Regt.	,,
,,	5	O.C.,7th ,,	,,
,,	6	O.C.,8th ,,	,,
,,	7	O.C.,15th ,,	,,
,,	8	O.C.,Bde.Trench Mortar Batty.	,,
,,	9	O.C.,Bde.Ammunition Reserve.	,,
,,	10	O.C.,8th Seaforths.	,,
,,	11	O.C.,10th Gordons.	,,
,,	12	G.O.C.,141st Infantry Bde.(for infn.)	,,
,,	13	G.O.C.,142nd do, ,,	,,

46
PUBLIC RECORD

SECRET.

Copy No.....9..

OPERATION ORDER NO.21

140th Infantry Brigade.

29th July, 1915.

1. The 140th Infantry Brigade will relieve the 141st Infantry Brigade in X Section on the night of July 30th-31st, 1915.

2. The 8th Battalion London Regiment will relieve the 20th Battalion London Regiment in X1, Headquarters Quality Street.

The 15th Battalion London Regiment will relieve the 19th Battalion London Regiment in X2, Headquarters Quality Street.

The 6th Battalion London Regiment will relieve the 18th Battalion London Regiment in LE PHILOSOPHE.

The 7th Battalion London Regiment will relieve the 17th Battalion London Regiment in LE PHILOSOPHE.

3. The 8th Battalion London Regiment (less 1 Company) will be met by guides of the 20th Battalion London Regiment at Headquarters X1, Quality Street, at 9.30p.m.

The 15th Battalion London Regiment will be met by guides of the 19th Battalion London Regiment at Headquarters X2, Quality Street, at 10.15p.m.

The 6th Battalion London Regiment will relieve the 18th Battalion London Regiment at LE PHILOSOPHE, leading relief party to leave MAZINGARBE at 8.30p.m.

The 17th Battalion London Regiment will relieve the 7th Battalion London Regiment at MAROC, which, as soon as relieved by 17th Battalion will proceed direct to LE PHILOSOPHE.

1 Company of the 8th Battalion London Regiment will relieve the garrison of the Keeps E,F,G and H, commencing at 4.30p.m., at 15 minute intervals between platoons. O.C.this Company will report to O.C.20th Battalion London Regiment, Headquarters Quality Street, at 9.30a.m.tomorrow.

4. O.C.8th Battalion London Regiment will arrange for guides to meet billeting party of the 20th Battalion at the Church at MAZINGARBE at 4.0p.m.

O.C.15th Battalion London Regiment will arrange for guides to meet billeting party of the 19th Battalion at the Church at MAZINGARBE at 4.0p.m.

O.C.6th Battalion London Regiment will arrange for guides to meet billeting party of the 18th Battalion London Regiment at MAZINGARBE Church at 4.0p.m.

O.C.7th Battalion will send a billeting party to Headquarters 17th Battalion at 4.0p.m. and a similar party of 17th Battalion will report at Headquarters 7th Battalion at the same time.

O.C.6th Battalion will send a billeting party to Headquarters 18th Battalion at 4.0p.m.

5. The relief of Machine Guns will be carried out under arrangements to be made by Brigade Machine Gun Officers of the 140th and 141st Infantry Brigades. The Brigade Machine Gun Officer will meet the Machine Gun Officer of the 141st Infantry Brigade at Headquarters 20th Battalion London Regiment at 9.30a.m.tomorrow.

6. The No.3 Trench Mortar Battery will be attached for rations to the 8th Battalion London Regiment from July 31st inclusive. The personnel consists of 1 Officer and 23 Other ranks.

7. The Brigade Trench Mortar Battery will be formed under Lieut.CULVERWELL, 7th Battalion, who will make the necessary arrangements with Officers Commanding Battalions. It will be attached for

rations

47

rations to the 15th Battalion. O.C.Trench Mortar Battery will meet the O.C.141st Trench Mortar Battery at Headquarters, X2 tomorrow at 9.30a.m.

8. Trench Stores (including VERMOREL SPRAYERS) will be taken over and receipts given.

9. Captain Gaze, 15th Battalion London Regiment will take over the Brigade Reserve of S.A.A.situated at Quality Street.

10. Battalion Transport will remain in its present situations.

11. Brigade Headquarters will move from NOEUX LES MINES to MAZINGARBE at 9.30p.m.

12. Battalions will report relief to Brigade Headquarters at CHATEAU MAZINGARBE immediately on completion.

13. The Dressing Station is situated at the Brewery, MAZINGARBE.

14. Ration wagons will be brought up on July 30th so that rations may be issued before Battalions move off. Wagons will move singly with at least 300 yds.distance between wagons.

15. O.C.Battalions will arrange for as many Company and Platoon Commanders as possible to visit the lines of the Units they are relieving during tomorrow morning.

16. Brigade Grenadier Company will be relieved under arrangements to be made by O.C.Grenadier Companies.

J H Westley

Captain,
Brigade Major,
140th Infantry Brigade.

Issued typewritten at 7.30p.m.

Copy No.		
1	War Diary	
2	Operation Order File.	
3	G.O.C.47th Division	By Signal Section.
4	G.O.C.141st Infantry Brigade.	,,
5	G.O.C.142nd ,,	,,
6	G.O.C.1st Division	,,
7	O.C.6th Bn.London Regt.	,,
8	O.C.7th ,,	,,
9	O.C.8th ,,	,,
10	O.C.15th ,,	,,
11	O.C.,Bde.Amm.Reserve	,,
12	O.C.,Bde.Trench Mortar Batty.	,,

48

OC. 8th Bn

SECRET.

Copy No.

29

142nd INFANTRY BRIGADE.

Operation Order No.24.

1. The 142nd Inf Bde will relieve the 140th Inf.Bde.in Section X on the night of 28th/29th June.
The G.O.C. is placing the 8th Battn.at the disposal of this Brigade for use as Brigade Reserve.

2. The 22nd Battn willrelieve the 6th Battn in Section X 1. Guides of the 6th Battn will meet the 22nd Battn.Company Officers at 5.pm.and the Battn at 8.30.p.m.at the West end of communication trench No.12 (G.20 c 1.7).
(X 1.Three Coys.firing line and supports-Hd Qrs.and one Coy.Local Reserve.)
Billetting party of the 6th Battn will be at MAZINGARBE Church at 5.p.m.to take over billets of the 22nd Battn.

3. The 23rd and 24th Battns.will relieve the 7th Battn.in Section X 2. Guides of the 7th Battn.will meet the 23rd and 24th Battn. Company Officers at 5.pm. and the Battn at 9.30.p.m.at(G.20 c 1.7).
(X 2.Two Companies 23rd Battn.and one Coy.24th Battn.firing line and supports-Hd Qrs.of both units and one Coy.24th Battn.local reserve
Order of March - 23rd Battn.
24th Battn.
Starting Point - Monument NOEUX LES MINES - 8.30.p.m.
Billetting party of the 15th Battn.will be at NOEUX LES MINES Church at 5.p.m. to take over billets of the 23rd and 24th Battns.

4. The 21st Battn will relieve the 8th Battn.at PHILOSPHE arriving there at 8.p.m. and will be in Brigade Reserve.
Billetting party of the 21st Battn. will be at the 8th Battn.Hdqrs at 5.p.m.
Billetting party of the 7th Battn.will be at MAZINGARBE Church at 5.p.m. to take over billets of the 21st Battn.

5. The 8th Battn. will relieve the 15th Battn.(Hdqrs and two Coys. MAZINGARBE-two Coys PHILOSPHE) under arrangements made by G.O.C. 140th Inf. Bde.

6. First line transport (Less cookers,water carts and medical carts) of both Brigades will remain in their present positions.

7. Brigade S.A.A.Reserve - Fosse No.7.

8. There is a Trench Mortar Battery of 1½"mortars under Lieut.Fairbairn R.F.A.in X 1 and X 2,and the Brigade Trench Mortar Battery under Lieut Lodge will be in X 1.
The 22nd Battn will arrange for rations for these batteries.

9. Units are reminded that the use of the new road in MAZINGARBE running on the East side of the line of village between the CHATEAU and LE SAULCHOY FERME is forbidden for all except necessary traffic.

10. Brigade Headquarters will move to MAZINGARBE from 5.p.m.tomorrow.

11. Reliefs of M.G.Sections will be carried out under the orders issued by B.M.G.Officers of the 140th and 142nd Inf.Bdes.

Issued at 3.45.p.m.27/6/15.

H Trevor
Major.
Brigade Major.

Copy No.1.Operation Order File.
" 2.47th (Lon)Div.
" 3.21st Bn.
" 4.22nd Bn.
" 5.23rd Bn.
" 6.24th Bn.
" 7.O.C.Signal Section.
Copy.No.8. B.M.G.O.
Copy.No.9. 140th Inf.Bde.
Copy.No.10.141st Inf.Bde.

SECRET. Copy No. 7

142nd INFANTRY BRIGADE

Operation Order - Number 26.

---

1. The 21st Battn. will relieve the 22nd Battn. in Section X 1 on the night of July 6th/7th., commencing at 9 p.m. under arrangements made by C. O's.
On relief the 22nd Battn. will be in the same distribution as the 21st Battn.
The garrison of the keeps and the company at disposal of O.C. Sub-section X 2 may be changed during daylight.

2. The 23rd Battn. will relieve the 24th Battn. in Section X 2 tonight under arrangements made by C. O's concerned.

3. The 20th Battn. will relieve the 8th Battn. in this Brigade reserve at PHILOSOPHE tonight.
C. O. 20th Battn. will inform this Headquarters as soon as it has taken over from the 8th Battn.

4. Trench Stores will be handed over; receipts given and taken, and inventories brought up to date.

5. In no case will troops being relieved leave their ground before the arrival of their reliefs.
Reports will be made to this office when reliefs are completed.

W. E. Trevor

Major,
Brigade Major,
142nd Inf. Bde.

6/7/16.

Issued at 11 a.m.

Copy No. 1. File.
2. 47th (London) Divn.
3. 21st. Bn.
4. 22nd. Bn.
5. 23rd. Bn.
6. 24th . Bn.
7. 8th. Bn.
8. 20th. Bn.
9. 141st. Inf. Bde. (for information)
10. 1st Brigade.

PUBLIC RECORD
OFFICE

51

140th Bde.

47th Div.

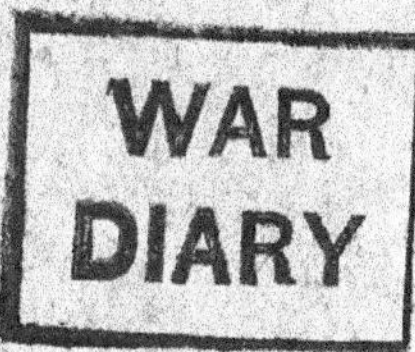

1/8th L O N D O N REGT.

AUGUST

1 9 1 5

Attached.
140th Inf Bde.
O.O. Nos. 22
and 23

On His Majesty's Service.

121/6695.

47th Division

1/8th London Regt

Vol VI

1 – 31. 8. 15

Nil

54

SECRET.

140TH INFANTRY BRIGADE.

15

Preliminary notice of relief.

The 6th and 7th Battalions London Regiment will be relieved on the night of the 2nd/3rd August by Units of the 45th Infantry Brigade, and will move into billets at LAPUGNOY.

The 8th and 15th Battalions will be relieved on the night of the 3rd/4th August by Units of the 45th Infantry Brigade, and will move into billets at LABEUVRIERE.

Billeting parties of all Battalions will be required to report at Brigade Headquarters, MAZINGARBE at 7.30a.m. on the 2nd August, prior to proceeding to the new billeting area.

The Trench Mortar Battery will continue to be attached to the 15th Battalion for billets and rations.

The Brigade Grenadier Company will be rationed by Units till night of August 3rd. After that date they will be accommodated and rationed by the 8th Battalion.

Further instructions will be issued later.

J H Wortley

Captain,
Brigade Major,
140th Infantry Brigade.

BRIGADE OFFICE
No. Bm. 4/26
31 JUL. 1915
140TH INFANTRY BRIGADE

Operation orders No.22

For paragraph 10 substitute the following:-

10. Arrangements must be made to bring up necessary wagons at intervals to loading-up points, where they must be carefully screened from view prior to departure of Units. Remainder of transport will move by the nearest route as under:-

6th and 7th Battalions at 10. 0p.m. on Aug.2nd to LAPUGNOY.
8th and 15th do. at 10.15p.m. on Aug.3rd to LABEUVRIERE.

S E C R E T.

Copy No......6...

OPERATION ORDER NO.22

140th Infantry Brigade.

1st August,1915.

1. The Brigade will be relieved by the 45th Infantry Brigade in Section X on the nights 2nd/3rd and 3rd/4th August,1915.

2. On relief, the Brigade will be billeted as under:-

Brigade Headquarters	LABEUVRIERE.
6th and 7th Battalions Lon.Regt.	LAPUGNOY.
8th and 15th do,	LABEUVRIERE.
Trench Mortar Battery	LABEUVRIERE.
Brigade Grenadier Company	LABEUVRIERE.

Units will move to their billets by the following route:- BETHUNE - LENS Road to road junction F.27.c., LA BOURSE, VAUDRICOURT, HESDIGNEUL, GOSNAY.

All moves taking place by daylight East of the line VAUDRICOURT-HOUCHIN-BARLIN will be by parties, not exceeding one platoon at 3 minute intervals.

Units may halt for a meal at any convenient point on their route West of the above line.

3. On the evenings of August 2nd and 3rd, the NOEUX LES MINES - MAZINGARBE road will be closed to all traffic at the NOEUX LES MINES end from 8.30p.m. to 9.30p.m., and from 8.0p.m. to 10p.m. at the MAZINGARBE end, to allow of the passage of infantry units of 15th Division.

4. Time Table of reliefs as per schedule attached. Every precaution must be taken in order to avoid observation during the process of these reliefs. Completion of reliefs to be at once reported to Brigade Headquarters.

5. The relief of the Machine Guns will be carried out under arrangements to be made between the Brigade Machine Gun Officers of the 140th and 45th Infantry Brigades.

6. No.3 Trench Mortar Battery will remain in X1 Section, and will come under the command of the G.O.C.,45th Infantry Brigade.

7. Three - 95mm.Trench Mortars with ammunition will be handed over on August 3rd, the remainder will be taken away under arrangements to be made by Officer i/c Trench Mortar Battery.

8. All trench stores will be handed over and receipts taken which will be forwarded to this office.

A list of all trench stores including bombs, ammunition, Vermorel Sprayers, etc. will be forwarded to this office by 4.0p.m. on August 4th.

9. The Grenadier Platoons of the 6th and 7th Battalions will march with their units to LAPUGNOY. They will join the remainder of the Brigade Grenadier Company on its arrival at LABEUVRIERE on the morning of August 4th.

~~10. Transport will accompany Units. Arrangements must be made to bring up necessary wagons at intervals to loading-up points, where they must be carefully screened from view prior to departure of Units.~~

See attached slip

11.

11. Captain Laurie, 7th Battalion London Regiment will be in charge of Brigade Billeting parties, which will assemble at 7.30 a.m. on August 2nd at Brigade Headquarters, MAZINGARBE.

12. Brigade Headquarters will close at MAZINGARBE on completion of reliefs and will open at LABEUVRIERE on arrival there.

J H Westley

Captain,
Brigade Major,
140th Infantry Brigade.

Issued typewritten at

Copy No.1	War Diary.		
,, 2	Operation Order File.		
,, 3	G.O.C., 47th (London) Division.	By Signal Section.
,, 4	O.C., 6th Bn.Lon.Regt.	,,
,, 5	O.C., 7th do.	,,
,, 6	O.C., 8th do.	,,
,, 7	O.C., 15th do.	,,
,, 8	O.C., Trench Mortar Battery	,,
,, 9	O.C., Bde.Grenadier Company	,,
,, 10	G.O.C., 45th Infantry Brigade	,,
,, 11	O.C., No.3 Trench Mortar Battery	,,

140th Infantry Brigade.

SCHEDULE OF RELIEFS.

Hour.	Date.	Unit to be relieved.	Relieving Unit of 45th Inf.Bde. and present position.	Billeting area on relief.	Hour and place of arrival of 45th Inf.Bde. billeting parties.	Place where guides are to be sent (4 per company).	Time.	Remarks.
	Night Aug.2/3	6th Bn.Lon.Regt.	13th Royal Scots BEUVRY.	LAPUGNOY.	5.0p.m. H.Q.6th Battn.	¼ mile N.W.of PHILOSOPHE on LENS-BETHUNE road.	p.m. 9.15	
	do.	7th Bn.Lon.Regt.	11th Argyle and Sutherlands. ANNEQUIN.	do.	5.0p.m. H.Q.7th Battn.	do.	10.0	
8.0a.m. to 1.0p.m.	Aug.3rd	8th Bn.Lon.Regt.	13th Royal Scots	PHILOSOPHE (vacated by 13th Royal Scots)	By arrangements between * O.C.Battalions concerned.			* An officer of 13th Ryl.Scots will report to O.C.8th Lon.Regt.on afternoon of Aug.2nd. Keeps G & H will be relieved during the afternoon by 11th Arg.& Sutherlands.
1.0p.m. to 6.0p.m.	Aug.3rd	15th Bn.Lon.Regt.	11th Argyle and Sutherlands.	PHILOSOPHE (vacated by 11th Arg.& S'lands.)	do.	do. /		/ An officer of 11th Arg.& Sutherlands will report to O.C. 15th Bn.on afternoon of Aug.2nd
	Night Aug.3/4	15th Bn.Lon.Regt.	7th Scots Fus. HESDIGNEUL.	LABEUVRIERE	5.0p.m. H.Q.15th Battn.	¼ mile N.W.of PHILOSOPHE on LENS-BETHUNE road.	9.30	
	Night Aug.3/4	8th Bn.Lon.Regt.	6th Camerons MAROC	LABEUVRIERE	~~XXX~~ 4.0p.m. H.Q.8th Battn.	½ mile S. of PHILOSOPHE on Philosophe-Grenay road.	9.15	

58

140th INFANTRY BRIGADE.

Working Parties for night of 1st-2nd August, 1915.

Battn.	Strength.	Tools.	Place where to report.	Time.	Place of drawing tools previously.	Work to be done.
7th	3 Officers and 200 men.	100 picks and 100 shovels.	H.Q. 8th Battalion.	9.0 p.m.	Brigade Headquarters.	Deepening Trench 9.
7th	1 Officer and 75 men.	50% picks and 50% shovels.	do.	8.45p.m.	Advanced R.E.Stores.	Traverses on Trench 6. 500 sandbags required.
6th	2 Officers and 100 men.	do.	do.	8.50p.m.	do.	Communication trenches between A & B Lines.
6th	2 Officers and 150 men.	do.	H.Q. 15th Battalion.	9.15p.m.	do.	~~Deepening~~ Work on Firing Trench and Support in X.2.
6th	1 Officer and 50 men.	do.	do.	9.30p.m.	do.	Deepening Communication Trench in X.2.

NOTE. All tools, except Brigade tools to be returned on completion of work. Brigade tools to be returned tomorrow by 11 a.m.

Captain,
Brigade Major,
140th Infantry Brigade.

59

O.C. 8th Lon Regt.

SECRET. No. 7

140th INFANTRY BRIGADE.

MACHINE GUNS.

Reference Operation Order No.22, para.5.

---

1. The Machine Guns of the 140th Infantry Brigade will be relieved by those of the 45th Infantry Brigade on August 3rd.

2. The B.M.G.O., 45th Infantry Brigade, will arrange for all his guns and personnel to be in QUALITY STREET by 1.30 a.m. August 3rd. All transport must be clear of QUALITY STREET by 2 a.m.

Guides of the 140th Infantry Brigade will be at the Church at MAZINGARBE as follows:-

6th Battalion at	11.0 p.m.	to meet	6th Camerons.
7th ,,	11.30 p.m.	,,	7th Scots Fusiliers.
8th ,,	10.0 p.m.	,,	13th Royal Scots.
15th ,,	10.30 p.m.	,,	11th Argyle & Sutherlands.

These guides will conduct the Battalions as above to LE PHILOSOPHE, where the S.A.A. carts will be left; they will then conduct the limbers to QUALITY STREET, where guns and equipment will be unpacked. After the unpacking, the guides will conduct the limbers to their position at LE PHILOSOPHE, and the horses to MAZINGARBE. Until the horses of the 140th Infantry Brigade move, the Corporals i/c of limbers of the 45th Infantry Brigade will arrange with the Corporals of the 140th Infantry Brigade for the necessary accommodation.

Section Officers will arrange for the accommodation of the guns and personnel of the 45th Infantry Brigade in QUALITY STREET until the guides report as in para. 3.

3. One guide per gun of the 140th Infantry Brigade will conduct the Machine Gun Sections of the 45th Infantry Brigade to their trench positions, leaving QUALITY STREET as follows:-

6th Camerons	at 3.30 a.m. to Keeps E & F.
7th Scots Fusiliers	at 3.45 a.m. to Keeps G & H.
13th Royal Scots	at 3.0 a.m. to Sub-section X.1.
11th Argyle & Sutherlands	at 3.15 a.m. to Sub-section X.2.

4. Section Officers of 140th Infantry Brigade will arrange to meet their respective relieving Officers as soon as the latter enter the trenches.

Before withdrawing their guns and personnel, Section Officers must ensure beyond all possibility of doubt that the Machine Gun Sections of the incoming Brigade are fully conversant with their duties and the general tactical situation.

5. Machine Gun Sections of the 140th Infantry Brigade will leave QUALITY STREET as follows:-

6th Battalion at	6.0 a.m.	7th Battalion at	6.15 a.m.
8th ,,	6.30 a.m.	15th ,,	6.45 a.m.

and will proceed to billets at LE PHILOSOPHE where they will breakfast.

6. All reserve S.A.A. forming trench stores (at least 3000 rounds per gun) will be handed over.

7. There must be at least 300 yards between limbers and S.A.A. carts.

8. All guides must be fully informed by the Section Officers as to the precautions to be taken by the 45th Infantry Brigade against attracting shell fire during the move from MAZINGARBE to the trenches.

9. The above times must, as far as possible, be strictly adhered to, with the exception of Section Officers, who, if they have not finished showing the incoming Section Officers the positions by the appointed

hour, may remain in the trenches until they have done. Should, however, the enemy show any activity, the relief will be temporarily suspended, and a message to this effect sent to the B.M.G.O., 140th Brigade.

10. As soon as reliefs are complete, Section Officers will inform their respective B.M.G.O's.

Captain,
Brigade Machine Gun Officer,
140th Infantry Brigade.

Copy No. 1	...	M.G.O., 6th Bn. London Regiment.	
,, 2	...	M.G.O., 7th Bn.	,,
,, 3	...	M.G.O., 8th Bn.	,,
,, 4	...	M.G.O., 15th Bn.	,,
,, 5	...	O.C. 6th Bn.	,,
,, 6	...	O.C. 7th Bn.	,,
,, 7	...	O.C. 8th Bn.	,,
,, 8	...	O.C. 15th Bn.	,,
,, 9	...	B.M.G.O., 45th Infantry Brigade.	
,, 10	...	File.	

AFTER ORDER.

11. The Machine Gun Sections will move from LE PHILOSOPHE and rejoin their Battalions as follows:-

6th Battalion at	will be advised later	leaving at	8.30 p.m.
7th ,,		,,	8.45 p.m.
8th ,,		,,	9.0 p.m.
15th ,,		,,	9.15 p.m.

Limbers and S.A.A. carts will move at 3 minute intervals, the Sections being equally distributed behind each.

Route to be followed:- BETHUNE-LENS road to road junction F.27.c - LABOURSE-VAUDRICOURT-HESDIGNEUL-GOSNAY.

Section Officers may arrange to rendezvous and halt for a meal at any convenient point on their route WEST of the line VAUDRICOURT-HOUCHIN-BARLIN.

12. Acknowledge.

M.G. 293.

Issued at 11.0 a.m.
2nd August, 1915.

60

SECRET.

30

PRELIMINARY OPERATION ORDER.

24th August, 1915.

1. The 47th (London) Division will take over Section "W" (less that portion of W.3 North of BOYAU 80 inclusive) from the 15th Division. The 140th Infantry Brigade will relieve the 46th Infantry Brigade in this Section.

2. In order to fit in with the revised billeting arrangements in the Corps reliefs will take place as follows:-

Night August 25th/26th.

The 5th London Battalion, now at LES BREBIS, will relieve the Battalion of the 46th Brigade in W.1.

The 8th London Battalion, now at LABOURSE, will relieve the Battalion of the 46th Brigade in Brigade Reserve at LES BREBIS.

These two Battalions will come under the command of the G.O.C. 46th Brigade.

One Battalion 141st Infantry Brigade will move from HOUCHIN to LES BREBIS and take over the billets at present occupied by the 8th Battalion.

Night August 26th/27th.

The remainder of the 140th Infantry Brigade will relieve the remainder of the 46th Brigade, moving via HESDIGNEUL, HOUCHIN and NOEUX LES MINES.

3. On the nights of August 25th/26th and 26th/27th the road from NOEUX LES MINES to MAZINGARBE will be kept clear of traffic at the NOEUX LES MINES end from 7 to 8 p.m. for the passage of the 47th Division troops. These troops will not move East of the Bridge in L.20.b.9.10 before 7 p.m.

On night August 25th/26th the Battalion of the 141st Infantry Brigade will follow the Battalion of the 140th Infantry Brigade.

Movements by daylight East of the line HOUCHIN-VAUDRICOURT will be by parties not exceeding a platoon and at 300 yards interval.

The Battalions of the 140th Infantry Brigade moving from LABEUVRIERE may halt for a meal West of HOUCHIN.

Captain,
Brigade Major,
140th Infantry Brigade.

31 J.H.

SECRET. **140th INFANTRY BRIGADE.** Copy No. 9...

28th August, 1915.

Reference Operation Orders No.23, para.4.

1. The Machine Gun Sections of the 140th Infantry Brigade will relieve those of the 46th Infantry Brigade in W.Section on the nights of August 25/27.

2.	6th Battn.Lon.Regt.will relieve		7th K.O.S.B.	in	W.3
	7th	do.	do. Royal Scots	in	KEMP S
	8th	do.	do. Scot.Rifles	in	W.1
	15th	do.	do. 12th H.L.I.	in	W.2

3. Billets will be handed over as in Para.2.

4. Machine Gun Sections will move to LES BREBIS with their Battalions.

5. Guides of 46th Infantry Brigade will be at LES BREBIS Church as follows:-

6th Bn.Lon.Regt.	at	9.0p.m.	on 25th	August.
8th do.	at	8.0p.m.	25th	do.
7th do.	at	9.30p.m.	26th	do.
15th do.	at	8.30p.m.	26th	do.

6. The 6th Battn.M.G.Section will move to Billets on night of 25th August and will proceed to the trenches during the day of 26th August under arrangements to be made by the B.M.G.O.,46th Infantry Brigade.

7. Distribution of 7th Battalion Guns:-
KEMP A ... 1 Gun.
,, C ... 2 Guns.
,, D ... 1 Gun.

8. 2 Limbers and 1 S.A.A.Cart per Battalion will remain close to Billets.

9. Horses and remaining S.A.A.Carts will return to their Battn. Transport Lines.

10. Sections will be rationed by their Battalions.

11. Reserve S.A.A.in trenches will be taken over.

12. Reliefs every 4 days.

13. Section Officers will advise B.M.G.O.as soon as reliefs are complete.

14. Acknowledge.

E.W.Hughes

MG/327.

Captain,
Brigade Machine Gun Officer,
140th Infantry Brigade.

Issued typewritten at 10.0a.m.

Copy No. 1	File.			
,, 2	M.G.O.6th Battn.	Copy No.6	B.M.G.O.,46th Inf.Bde.
,, 3	M.G.O.7th ,,	,, 7	O.C.6th Battn.
,, 4	M.G.O.8th ,,	,, 8	O.C.7th ,,
,, 5	M.G.O.15th ,,	,, 9	O.C.8th ,,
		,, 10	O.C.15th ,,

63

SECRET.

OPERATION ORDER No.23

140th Infantry Brigade.

24th August, 1915.

1. The 140th Infantry Brigade will relieve the 46th Infantry Brigade in "W" Section (less that portion of W.3 North of BOYAU 29 inclusive).

2. Reliefs will take place as follows:- August 25th.
The 8th Bn.London Regiment will relieve the 10th Bn.Scottish Rifles commencing at 4p.m., at which hour the leading company will cross the LES BREBIS level crossing, companies moving thence at one hour intervals by half platoons, via the railway cutting West of LES BREBIS-GRENAY road and the cutting leading to FOSSE 5.
Guides of the 10th Scottish Rifles will meet leading company of 8th London Regiment at LES BREBIS level crossing at 4p.m.
Night August 25th-26th.
The 6th Bn.LondonRegiment will leave LABOURSE at 7 p.m. and will move by the shortest route to N.& S.MAROC where they will be in Brigade Reserve.
Transport will move via NOEUX LES MINES and will clear the bridge at L.20.b.9.10 by 7.30p.m.
Parties will be sent to arrange for billets in N.& S.MAROC during the afternoon.
Night August 26th-27th.
The 6th Bn.London Regiment will relieve the 7th K.O.S.B's in W.3, under arrangements to be made by O.C.Units concerned. The relief will commence at 6.30p.m.
The 15th Bn.London Regiment will relieve the 12th Highland Light Infantry in W.2. Guides will meet leading company at LES BREBIS level crossing at 8 p.m.
The 7th Bn.London Regiment will occupy the billets vacated by the 6th Bn.London Regiment in N.& S.MAROC and will be in Brigade Reserve.
Billeting parties to report at Headquarters 6th Bn.London Regiment at 3 p.m. on August 26th.

3. On the nights of August 25th-26th and 26th-27th the road from NOEUX LES MINES will be kept clear of traffic at the NOEUX LES MINES end from 7 to 8 p.m. for the passage of 47th Divisional troops. No troops will move East of the bridge in L.20.b.9.10 before 7 p.m.
Movements by daylight East of the line HOUCHIN-VAUDRICOURT will be by parties not exceeding a platoon and at 300 yds. intervals.
The 15th and 7th Bns.London Regiment will march via HOUCHIN and NOEUX LES MINES, and will halt for a meal just West of HOUCHIN.
The leading Platoon of the 15th Battalion will pass the bridge in L.20.b.9.10 at 7 p.m., and the 7th Battalion will follow the 15th Battalion.

4. The relief of Machine Guns will be carried out under arrangements made by the Brigade Machine Gun Officers of the 140th and 46th Brigades.

5. No.8 Trench Mortar Battery (2 Officers and 28 men) will be attached to the 8th Bn.London Regiment for rations.

6. The Brigade Trench Mortar Battery will march with the 15th Bn. London Regiment and will remain attached to that Battalion until further orders.
O.C.Battery will take over guns on charge of Battalion in W.1 Section.

64

7. Battalion Grenadier Platoons will return to duty with their Battalions tomorrow and will accompany them to the trenches.

8. Trench stores (including Vermorel Sprayers) will be carefully checked and receipts given. Lists of stores taken over to be sent to Brigade Office by 5 p.m. on the day following the relief.

9. Captain GAZE, 15th Bn.London Regiment, will take over the Brigade S.A.A.Reserve, situated near the Advanced R.E.Store at SOUTH MAROC, at 7 p.m.on the 26th August.

10. The Dressing Station will be at LES BREBIS.

11. Brigade Headquarters will move from LABEUVRIERE to LES BREBIS at 9 p.m. on 26th August.

12. The completion of all reliefs will be notified by priority telegram to the 46th Infantry Brigade and repeated to the 140th Infantry Brigade.

13. All Units will be under the command of the G.O.C.46th Infantry Brigade until relief is completed on the night August 26th-27th.

J H Westley

Captain,
Brigade Major,
140th Infantry Brigade.

Issued typewritten at 9.30p.m.

Copy No.			
Copy No.	1	War Diary.	
,,	2	Operation Order File.	
,,	3	O.C. 6th Bn.London Regt.	Signal Service.
,,	4	O.C. 7th do.	do.
,,	5	O.C. 8th do.	do.
,,	6	O.C.15th do.	do.
,,	7	G.O.C.,47th (London) Division.	do.
,,	8	G.O.C.,46th Infantry Brigade.	do.
,,	9	G.O.C.,141st Infantry Brigade.	do.
,,	10	O.C. Trench Mortar Battery.	do.
,,	11	O.C. Grenadier Company.	do.
,,	12	O.C.Brigade Ammunition Reserve.	do.

65

67

140th Bde.
47th Division.

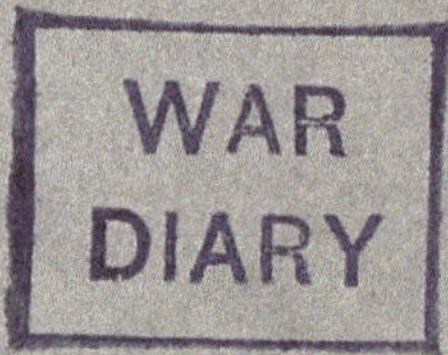

1/8th LONDON REGIMENT.

S E P T E M B E R

1 9 1 5

Attached:
Appendices.

3.

8th Bn London Rgt.
Post Office Rifles

War Diary Sept.

1st Bn remained in S. Marov
2nd The Bn was relieved in S Marov by the 23rd London Rgt & dug during the night in front of W2 Section.
At 3 am the Bn embussed & proceeded to HAILLICOURT & took over billets from the 21st Bn London Rgt.
3rd } The Bn rested at HAILLICOURT
4th }
5th The Bn to Brebis & took over the billets of the 7th Bn London Rgt.
6th The Bn employed digging
7. The Bn left before daylight for HAILLICOURT taking over the billets of the 15th Bn L.R.
8 }
9 }
10 } The Bn remained at HAILLICOURT
11 }
12 }
13 The Bn proceeded to LES BREBIS & took over the billets of the 7th Bn London Rgt.
14 Bn digging at Les BREBIS
15 — " —
16 Bn less No2 Coy left for HAILLICOURT & took over the billets of the 6th Bn

16. Lt G N Clarke rejoined for duty.
2/Lt W F Frye
2/Lt F G Bowman 5th Middlesex Rgt joined for duty on being attached to the Bn.

17 }
18 } The Bn remained at HAILLICOURT.

19 The Bn moved to Les BREBIS & took over the command of the 15th Bn London Rgt.

20 Bn digging at Les Brebis
Lt G N Clarke & 7 Riflemen wounded.
1 Rifleman killed.

21 The Bn returned to HAILLICOURT & took over the billets of the 15th Bn Rgt

22 The Bn digging at Les BREBIS

23 The Bn moved to billets at Noeux les Mines

24 The Bn moved at 7pm & by 2am 25th was in its position in the old fire trenches of W2 Section prior to the assault on the Double Crassier

25. At 6.30 am a slight wind being just sufficient to enable gas & smoke to have been used since 5.50 am the 6th & 7th Bn London Rgt left their trenches & successfully assaulted the Double Crassier & 1st & 2nd line of German trenches to the N.

The Bn immediately occupied the trenches vacated by these Bns & held themselves in readiness to support.

At am a German bombing counter attack seriously threatened the right flank of the 7th Bn & Lt Thomas & the Sections of 2 & 3 Coys were ordered up in support.

They succeeded in driving back the counter attack & in double blocking.

At am Nos 1 & 2 Coys were ordered to support the 7th Bn & they proceeded some 15 min later under Major Maxwell.

At 6pm No 3 & 1 MG Coy was sent to hold part of the line captured by the 6th Bn

At 8pm No 4 Coy 2 M Guns & Headquarters crossed & occupied a portion of the trenches occupied by the 7th Bn.

Lt Dugdale slightly wounded
7 Other ranks killed
32 — " — wounded
1 Missing

26 The Bn continued consolidating the position.

There was heavy fighting on the left flank all day when the Germans make a counterattack on the 15th DW.

Other Ranks 1 Killed 7 wounded.

27 ~~finished~~ The Bn. consolidated the position. In the evening these 2 Coy in moving into position after dark to occupy the double Crassier were met by bombers, whom they dispersed.

Wounded 17 Other Ranks

28th The Bn remained in the German Trenches taking over the whole of that part captured by the 7th Bn who withdrew at dusk.

The M-Gun Battery of the Brigade was broken up & Lt Stapylton joined with the 4 Guns.

No 3 Coy rejoined the Bn

Other Ranks 1 killed 10 wounded.

29th The Bn remained in its same position

30th The Bn was relieved after dark by a Bn of the 4th Maroc Bde & moved to Quality St

7 Other Ranks wounded.

Note

During the Operations commencing on the 25th the weather was mostly cold & wet & the roads & trenches were in a very bad state.

Robinson Capt & Adjt

2/10/15

H = HYDRANT.

T = TAP.

SP = STAND PIPE.

SV = STOP VALVE.

FOSSE No. 5.

CRASSIER

SAP 4

SAP 5

SAP 6

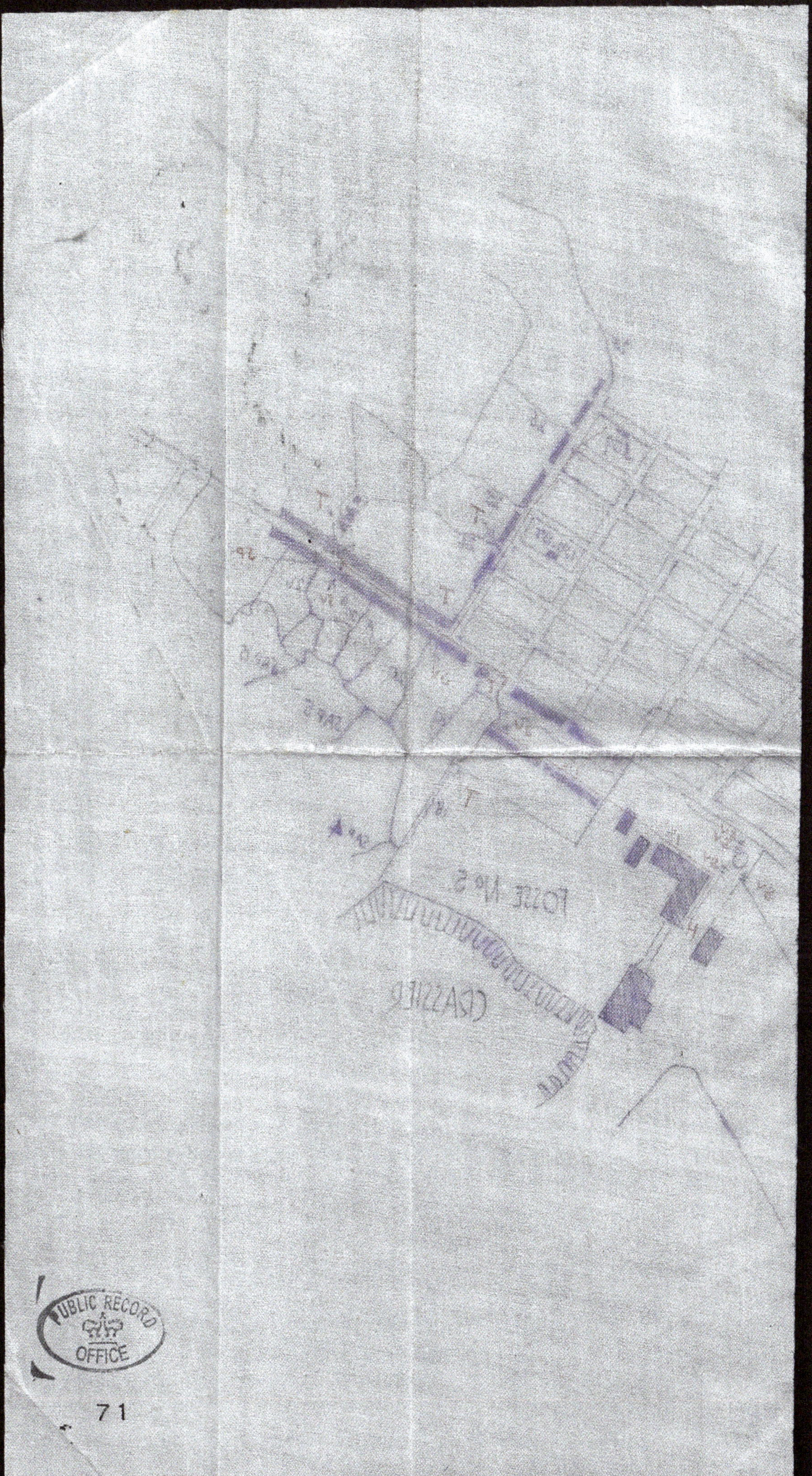

TWENTY NINTH DIV.

DARDANELLES.

MOBILISATION &
TRANSPORT.

BDE. DIARY,
88th Inf.
(contd).

13th. 67th arrived at STRATFORD o.A. & went into billets.

5/1st = 5th R Scots (TF)
4/29th = 4th Worcesters
44th = 1st Essex
67th = 2nd Hampshire

14th Jan. '15. Bde. H.Q. established at STRATFORD onA.

18th. 44th arrived at BANBURY from HARWICH & went into billets. Strength 25 & 893, and 7 horses.

27th. Br.Genl.H.E.Napier arrived & assumed command of Bde.

2nd Feb. 4/29th arrived from abroad - strength 23 & 946 - & went into billets at BANBURY.

4th. Capt. A.C.M.Sinclair Thompson arrived for duty as Staff Capt.

5th Mar. Went into new billets at WARWICK & LEAMINGTON. Bde. H.Q., 67th & 44th at WARWICK. 4/29th at LEAMINGTON.

8th. Received notice that 5/1st from EDINBURGH will join Bde. instead of 57th.

11th. 5/1st arrived & went into billets at LEAMINGTON.

20th. 67th & portion of remaining 3 Bns. entrained for AVONMOUTH DOCKS & embarked immediately on arrival.

21st. Bde. H.Q. & remainder of 4/29th, 44th, & 5/1st, proceed to AVONMOUTH DOCKS & embark as follows:-

s.s."Caledonia" Bde. H.Q. less transport, 44th less transp. 5/1st less transp. 1 Co. 4/29th

s.s."Aragon" 67th less 2 Cos & transp. 1 Co. 4/29th.

s.s."Melville" Transport of 44th, 5/1st, & 4/29th.

s.s."Southland" 4/29th less 2 Cos.

s.s."Manitou" 2 Cos. 67th. s.s."Campenella" Bde.H.Q. transp.

By this dividing of units from their transports, much inconvenience was caused

Distribution	No. 1 Coy Officers	No. 1 Coy Other Ranks	No. 2 Coy Officers	No. 2 Coy Other Ranks	No. 3 Coy Officers	No. 3 Coy Other Ranks	No. 4 Coy Officers	No. 4 Coy Other Ranks	Totals Officers	Totals Other Ranks
"A" Ration Strength.	10	219	5	187	6	195	8	179	29	780.
"B" Trench Strength										
(i) As Riflemen.	4	134	5	126	5	130	5	123	19	516
(ii) As Grenadiers		12		11	1	11		10	1	44
(iii) As Batt. M. Gun.		9		2		7	1	6	1	24
(iv) As Signallers		8		7		5		4		24.
(v) As Runners		5		6		4		5		20
(vi) As Stretcher Bearers		4		5		4		4		17
(vii) As Trench Mortar Batt.		6		3		2		2		13
(viii) As Bde. M. Gun Batt.	1	4		4		1		–	1	9.
(ix) Employed as Storemen		3		1		2		2		8.
(x) Bn. Headquarters	3	10		8		6	2	6	5	30
(xi) Pioneers.		4		2		2		3		11
Totals.	8	202	5	145	6	144	8	165	27	716
2nd & 3rd Echelon "C" Difference between "A" & "B"	2	17	–	12	–	21		14	2	64
Transport. Officer	1								1	–
Sergeant						1				1
Grooms		1		2		5		3		11
Drivers		5		3		3		4		15
Pack				2		3		3		8
Spare Horses.				1		3				4.
Brakesmen		2		2		1		2		7
Farrier & Cook						1		1		2
M. Gun Driver		2				1				3
M. Gun Pack		2								2
Divl. Mounted Orderly.						1				1
Bugle Sgt. (Post)		1								1
Orderly Room Clerk				1						1
Interpreter.		1								1
Quartermaster	1								1	
Ditto. Servant.		1								1
Regtl. Qmr. Sgt.				1						1
Qmr.'s Clerk.						1				1
Butcher.								1		1
Shoemakers.		2				1				3
Totals	2	17		12		21		14	2	64

PUBLIC RECORD
OF

74

140th Bde.

47th Div.

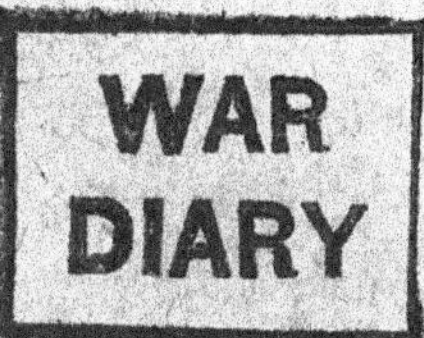

1/8th LONDON REGT.

OCTOBER.

1 9 1 5

Attached:
140th Inf. Bde
O.O. Nos. 31,
34, 35 and 36.
Map.

On His Majesty's Service.

47th Division

121/7384

1/8th London Regt.

Vol VIII

Oct 15

76

8th Bn London Regt.
(Post Office Rifles).
WAR DIARY October.

1st The Bn moved from QUALITY STREET to VERQUIN.

2nd
3rd
4th
5th } The Bn rested at VERQUIN

6th The Bn left VERQUIN and took up billets at NOEUX-LES-MINES.

7th The Bn remained at NOEUX-LES-MINES

8th The Bn, with rest of 140th Bde, was inspected by Lt Genl. Sir Henry Rawlinson G.O.C 4th Corps at 2-30 pm. At 6 p.m. Bn moved to billets at MAZINGARBE the Bde being moved up to support the 1st Divn. Draft of 70 other ranks joined from 7th Entrenching Bn.

9th
10th
11th } Bn remained at MAZINGARBE

12th Bn left its billets at MAZINGARBE and occupied the old British line, with its right resting on RED FLAG

13th Bn moved at 3-30 am to old British front line between LONE TREE and BOIS CARRE.
OR wounded 1

14th 2 Coys + 2 MGs moved at 3 am to old German front line under Major Maxwell. At 5-45 pm. Bn moved & took over part of new line held by 1st Bn Camerons, the

the Royal Sussex and Northamptonshire Regiments, all of 1st & 2nd Bdes, 1st Divn. G 18 b 86 - G 18 b 05

OR wounded 2

15th Bn remained in trenches.

OR killed 3, wounded 5

16th Bn remained in trenches. Draft of 38 OR. joined from 7th Entrenching Bn.

OR wounded 9.

17th Bn ~~was~~ remained in trenches, but was relieved in front line by 7th Bn, relief commencing 11-30 p.m. Bn took over support line vacated by 7th Bn

G 18 b 35 - G 18 c 45

2nd Lt. K.E.M. Gardiner killed; O.R. killed 1, wounded 7.

18th Bn remained in support line. Lt Col. J. Harvey recd. D.S.O.

19th }
20th } Bn remained in support line.

21st Bn relieved 7th Bn in front line trenches, relief commencing 8-30 pm.

22nd Bn remained in front line trenches. Lt. A. Thomas recd. Military Cross. OR. wounded 2.

23rd Bn was relieved by 23rd Bn, London Regt., relief commencing 6-15 pm., and moved to billets at PHILOSOPHE (CORONS DE MAZINGARBE). No 1 Coy garrisoned 4 Redoubts in Old German line. OR killed 1

24th Bn remained in billets at PHILOSOPHE

25th Bn remained in billets at PHILOSOPHE. No 4 Coy. relieved No 1 Coy in the Redoubts.

OR killed 2

26th } 27th } Bn remained in billets at PHILOSOPHE.

28th Bn remained in billets at PHILOSOPHE. A composite Coy. of 200 O.R. & 6 officers under command of Captain Alexander represented the Bn at an inspection by the King at LABUISSIERE.

29th Bn remained in billets at PHILOSOPHE. Capt. & Adj. T. H. P. Morris left the Bn to take over command of 9th Bn Rifle Brigade. O.R. killed 2.

30th Bn left its billets at PHILOSOPHE at 5-15 pm. and relieved 17th Bn London Regt in the A1 Sector - NE of LOOS H.31 A17 - G30 d 56 (vide Operation Orders of 30/X/15).

31st Bn remained in trenches. Front & right support lines were heavily shelled.

OR killed 1, wounded 12

—— " ——

[illegible]

1 November 1915

To accompany War Diary
October 1915

140th Infantry Brigade Operation Orders
Nos 31, 34, 35, 36

Map – Trench Map 36C NW 3 &
part of I 1/10,000

COPY No.4 ~~50~~

65

OPERATION ORDER No. 31

by

Brigadier General G.J.Cuthbert, C.B.

8th October, 1915.

1. The Brigade will move to MAZINGARBE this evening and will be in readiness to support either the 1st Division or the French 9th Corps.

2. Battalions will pass the LEVEL CROSSING L.14.c moving by platoons, at intervals, as under -

Brigade Headquarters	-	5.45 p.m.
6th Bn.Lon.Regt	- - -	6.0 p.m.
7th do.	- - -	6.20 p.m.
8th do.	- - -	6.40 p.m.
15th do.	- - -	7.0 p.m.

3. Officers Commanding Units will arrange for guides from the Billeting Parties to meet Battalions on their arrival at the CROSS ROAD L.22.d.

4. Transport will accompany Units.

5. Officers Commanding Units will report on arrival at MAZINGARBE.

6. Position of Brigade Headquarters will be notified later.

J H Weikley
Captain,
Brigade Major,
140th Infantry Brigade.

Issued at 2.30 p.m.

Copy No.	1	...	Operation Order File.		
,,	2	...	O.C. 6th	Bn. Lon. Regt.	By Signal Section.
,,	3	...	O.C. 7th	do.	do.
,,	4	...	O.C. 8th	do.	do.
,,	5	...	O.C. 15th	do.	do.

6 11 + 17

18 10. + 28

3 11 + 14 4 | 53

. 11 + 11

70

76

27

43

10 110 . 113 | 13

25 48 113 116 | 25

10 143 113 | 10

15 111 114

COPY No. 5

140th INFANTRY BRIGADE.

Operation Order No. 31.

11th October, 1915.

Reference Map 1/40,000 Sheet 36c.
1/10,000 Sheet 36c NW3.

1. The IVth Corps have been ordered to secure and consolidate the line of the LENS-LA BASSEE Road between the CHALK PIT (H.25.a.7.5) and about H.13.a.2.6.
The XIth Corps at the same time have been ordered to capture and hold FOSSE 8 and the QUARRIES, and establish a defensive flank North and East of these places.

2.(a) The 1st Division has been ordered to carry out the task allotted to the IVth Corps.
(b) It will seize the German trenches from about H.19.a.7.8 to about H.13.a.2.6.
(c) All the Artillery of the IVth Corps now in position will support this advance under orders to be issued by 1st Division, and will carry out a preliminary bombardment at a time to be notified later.
(d) Such gas and smoke as can be brought up in time will be discharged along the front to be attacked by 1st Division.
(e) The date and time of assault, and programme for the discharge of gas and smoke, will be issued later.
(f) After capture of the objective given in 2(b) above, the line of the LENS-LA BASSEE Road, from about H.13.a.2.6 as far South as the CHALK PIT in H.25.a, will be consolidated by the 1st Division.
(g) As soon as the objective given in 2(b) above has been captured, immediate steps will be taken to ascertain if HULLUCH is still held, with a view to taking advantage of any panic which may result from the gas attack.

3. The 47th Division moves into a position of readiness on night 12th-13th October; the 142nd Infantry Brigade occupying GRENAY Line and VERMELLES Branch between FINCHLEY ROAD (exclusive) and the BETHUNE-LENS Road; the 141st Infantry Brigade and the 1/4th Field Company R.E. being at MAZINGARBE.

4.(a) The Brigade will take up positions as under:-
15th Bn. London Regiment in old front system of trenches between G.28.a.8.5 and G.22.c.8.6 (both inclusive).
8th Bn. London Regiment in old front system of trenches between G.22.c.8.6 (exclusive) and G.22.a.8.5 (inclusive).
7th Bn. London Regiment in old front system of trenches between G.22.a.8.5 and G.16.d.6.4 (both exclusive).
6th Bn. London Regiment in Trenches 15 and 16 between BETHUNE-LENS Road and LE RUTOIRE ALLEY (exclusive).
Officers Commanding Units will report to Brigade Headquarters as soon as possible the positions selected for their Headquarters.
(b) Battalions will pass the Starting Point, LE SAULCHOY FARM, square L.17.d, moving by platoons at intervals, as under-
7th Battalion - ~~6.30 p.m.~~ 5.50 P.M.
× 8th ,, - ~~7.00 p.m.~~ 6.10 P.M.
15th ,, - ~~7.30 p.m.~~ 6.30 P.M.
The 6th Battalion will move into its allotted position at 9 p.m.

5.(a) Officers Commanding Units will arrange for routes to be reconnoitred and for guides of each company to have a knowledge of them.
After dark it would appear to be safe to move over the open.
(b) Companies will be distributed at the discretion of Officers

× The rear of the 15th Bn to clear the cross roads at L23b66 by 7-0 PM to allow passage of 142nd Inf Bde.

80

Commanding Battalions, who will ensure that areas allotted are held in sufficient strength. Sentries will be posted by all companies and at Battalion Headquarters, and a keen look-out kept for signals.

(c) The trenches are much damaged, and although small parties may move during the day, large numbers are immediately shelled.

During the night it would appear safe for troops to sleep outside the trenches.

6. Water carts will be taken up after dark, and arrangements should be made to dig them in so that they can be left near the trenches during the day, if O's C. Units so desire.

7. Transport will remain in its present positions in MAZINGARBE.

8. S.A.A. carts will be brigaded under Captain GAZE, 15th Battn. London Regiment, in the transport lines of the 15th Battalion.

Each Unit will send an orderly from its Transport Section at 6.30 p.m. to report and remain with Captain GAZE.

9. Grenadiers will carry 100 rounds of ammunition and 6 grenades on the man.

10. Brigade Headquarters will move at 6.30 p.m. to LE PHILOSOPHE, about square G.20.a.0.5, where reports will be sent as soon as units have occupied their allotted positions.

A H Wetley

Captain,
Brigade Major,
140th Infantry Brigade.

Issued typewritten at

Copy No.				
Copy No. 1	...	Operation Order File.		
,, 2	...	War Diary.		
,, 3	...	O.C. 6th Bn. Lon, Regt.		By Signal Section.
,, 4	...	O.C. 7th	do.	do.
,, 5	...	O.C. 8th	do.	do.
,, 6	...	O.C. 15th	do.	do.
,, 7	...	G.O.C. 1st Division.		do.
,, 8	...	G.O.C. 47th	do.	do.

3 - Ela

No 1. ESP

7 D.

SECRET. 140th INFANTRY BRIGADE. Copy No. 5

67

Operation Order No. 34.

21st October, 1915.

1. The Brigade will be relieved by the 142nd Infantry Brigade on the nights 22nd/23rd and 23rd/24th October, 1915.

2. On night 22nd/23rd

(a). 7th Battalion will be relieved by 21st Battalion.

Guides will meet companies of 21st Battalion at 6.30p.m. at LONE TREE and conduct them by HAY ALLEY to the trenches. Companies of 21st Battalion will move in with the company to occupy the left of the line leading, their right flank company in rear.

On relief 7th Battalion will move out by VENDIN ALLEY and will occupy old English 1st Line trenches (not the gas or assembly trenches) in squares G.16.b and d (excluding the part allotted to headquarters of 142nd Infantry Brigade).

(b). 6th Battalion will be relieved by 24th Battalion. ~~[illegible]~~. After relief, 6th Battalion will move into billets at MAZINGARBE. Guides of 6th Battn. will meet 24th Battn. at Cross Roads G.15.c at 7.30 p.m. and lead them to the trenches.

3. On night 23rd/24th

(a). 8th Battalion will be relieved by 23rd Battalion.

Guides will meet companies of 23rd Battalion at LONE TREE at 6.15p.m. and will conduct them via POSEN STREET to the trenches. On relief 8th Battalion will move out by HAY ALLEY to billets at PHILOSOPHE CORONS, finding a garrison of one platoon in each of the strong posts LENS ROAD [illegible]

[illegible]

[illegible]

LONE TREE REDOUBT [illegible]

The Machine Gun Section of R. Welsh Fus. forms part of the garrison of these points.

(b). 15th Battalion will be relieved by 22nd Battalion.

Guides will meet 22nd Battalion at LONE TREE at 7.30p.m., and will lead the companies by VENDIN ALLEY. On relief 15th Battalion will move out by sunken road alongside VENDIN ALLEY and will relieve 7th Battalion in trenches G.16.b and d. 7th Battalion, after relief, will move to MAZINGARBE.

(c). Grenadier Platoons of 22nd and 23rd Battalions will be met at LONE TREE one hour before the arrival of their battalions and will be taken to the posts held by grenadiers of 15th and 8th Battalions respectively, who will remain with them till all companies have completed their relief.

4. Relief of Machine Guns will be carried out under arrangements to be made by Brigade Machine Officers.

5. All trench stores, except periscopes, Very pistols and telescopic rifles, will be handed over and receipts taken.

6. Battalions to be billeted in MAZINGARBE will send representatives to report to Staff Captain at the Church at 2.30p.m. on Friday, 22nd October.

7. Completion of reliefs will be reported immediately to Brigade Headquarters. Brigade Headquarters will move to house near Church at MAZINGARBE, L.2?.c.?.? after completion of reliefs.

J H Whitley

Captain,
Brigade Major,
140th Infantry Brigade.

(over).

Issued at

Copy No.	1	Operation Order File.	
,,	2	War Diary.	
,,	3	O.C.6th Bn.Lon.Regt.	By Signal Service.
,,	4	O.C.7th do.	do.
,,	5	O.C.8th do.	do.
,,	6	O.C.15th do.	do.
,,	7	47th Division.	do.
,,	8	141st Infantry Brigade.	do.
,,	9	142nd do.	do.

82

Copy No. 5

68

140th INFANTRY BRIGADE.

Operation Order No. 88.

26th October, 1916.

1. The 8th Battalion will relieve the 15th Battalion in the old British front line trenches in squares G.16.b and d on October 27th, under arrangements to be made between Commanding Officers concerned.

The 8th Battalion will not move East of LE PHILOSOPHE before 6.30p.m.

On relief, the 15th Battalion will take over the billets of the 8th Battalion at MAZINGARBE.

2. The 7th Battalion will relieve the garrisons of the strong posts, now found by the 8th Battalion, on October 27th, as follows:-

LENS Road	G.34.a.5.9.	1 Platoon
65 metre Point Redoubt	G.28.b.5.2.	,,
NTH. LOOS AVENUE Redoubt	G.23.a.4.1.	,,
LONE TREE Redoubt	G.17.b.5.0.	,,

The relieving platoons will not move East of LE PHILOSOPHE before 6.0p.m.

Completion of reliefs to be reported to H.Q. 140th and 142nd Infantry Brigades.

Captain,
for Brigade Major,
140th Infantry Brigade.

Issued at 11.15 a.m.

Copy No.1	Operation Order File.		
,, 2	War Diary.		
,, 3	O.C.6th Bn.Lon.Regt.		By Signal Service,
,, 4	O.C.7th	do.	do.
,, 5	O.C.8th	do.	do.
,, 6	O.C.15th	do.	do.

SECRET.

Copy No. 5......

140th INFANTRY BRIGADE.

Operation Order No.36.

29th October, 1915.

1. The 140th Infantry Brigade will relieve the 141st Infantry Brigade in Section A on the nights 30th/31st Oct. and 31st Oct./ 1st Nov.

2. The 8th Battalion will relieve the 17th Battalion in A1 on the night of Oct.30th/31st. Guides will meet the 8th Battalion at the cross roads at G.34.b.3.1 at 6.0p.m.

The 7th Battalion will relieve the 20th Battalion in A3 on the night of Oct.30th/31st. Guides will be at cross roads at G.34.b.3.1 at 6.30p.m.

The 15th Battalion will relieve the 19th Battalion in A2 on the night of Oct.31st/Nov.1st. Guides will be at cross roads at G.34.b.3.1 at 6.0p.m.

The 6th Battalion will relieve the 18th Battalion in Brigade Reserve on the night Oct.31st/Nov.1st. Guides will be at cross roads at G.34.b.3.1. at 6.30p.m.

Reliefs will be carried out by Companies at 150yds. interval, moving in single file on each side of the road.

3. All snipers will go into the line on the night of 30th/31st October, under instructions to be issued by the Brigade Machine Gun Officer.

4. Machine Guns will be relieved under arrangements of Brigade Machine Gun Officers concerned.

5. Trench Stores, including Braziers and Steel helmets, will be taken over and receipts given, copies of which will be sent to Brigade Headquarters.

6. The G.O.C.,140th Infantry Brigade will assume command of A Section at 6.0p.m. on October 31st.

7. Brigade Headquarters will be situated at PHILOSOPHE, G.19.d.10.5.

8. The completion of reliefs will be reported to Brigade Headquarters.

Edward Orsattos [signature]
Captain,
for Brigade Major,
140th Infantry Brigade.

Issued at

Copy No.			
Copy No.1	Operation Order File.		
,, 2	War Diary.		
,, 3	O.C., 6th Bn.Lon.Regt.	By Signal Service.	
,, 4	O.C., 7th do.	do.	
,, 5	O.C., 8th do.	do.	
,, 6	O.C., 15th do.	do.	
,, 7	*141st Infantry Brigade.	do.	
,, 8	*142nd do.	do.	
,, 9	*47th (London) Division.	do.	

*For information.

84

86

87

www.ingramcontent.com/pod-product-compliance
Lightning Source LLC
Chambersburg PA
CBHW081531160426
43191CB00011B/1736

* 9 7 8 1 4 7 4 5 2 6 2 7 2 *